HUEY'S
GREATEST
HITS

HUEY'S GREATEST HITS

IAIN HEWITSON

PHOTOGRAPHY BY GREG ELMS
A SUE HINES BOOK ALLEN & UNWIN

First published in 2002

A Sue Hines Book
Allen & Unwin
83 Alexander Street
Crows Nest NSW 2065
Australia
Phone: (61 2) 8425 0100
Fax: (61 2) 9906 2218
Email: info@allenandunwin.com
Web: www.allenandunwin.com

National Library of Australia
Cataloguing-in-Publication entry:

Hewitson, Iain.
    Huey's greatest hits.
    Includes index.
    ISBN 1 86508 860 9.
    1. Cookery. I. Elms, Greg. II. Title.
    641.5

Designed by Andrew Cunningham – Studio Pazzo
Food styling by Virginia Dowzer
Index by Fay Donlevy
Typeset by Pauline Haas

Printed in Singapore by Imago

10 9 8 7 6 5 4 3

The author and publisher thank Country Road for their generous loan of the coloured Bistro mugs and bowls and white Como dinnerware used in the food photography.

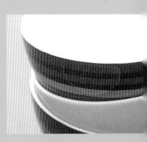

Contents

Thanks

To Ruth for all her help (and patience) and to Charlotte for sleeping through the night almost from day one.

To Sue and Andrea and the team at Allen & Unwin for all their support.
To Ruth A and all the crew at Tolarno.
To Virginia and Greg for making the food look great.
To my mates Mosh and Donnelly and everyone at Dreampool Productions.
To Rob, Noel, Pat, Travis and all other cameramen and soundies.

And of course, we mustn't forget Mr Moon.

Hi
Hewy – Baby!
We love your show
i have your books
ut my Mum wan
to report you to th
RSPCA for cruelty
THE TURKEY in y
pening credits.

HUEY'S
TOP TEN

The most requested recipes in no particular order

and just to prove I can't count

Introduction

You certainly don't need to be a rocket scientist to work out which recipes are a hit on a television cooking show, because about five minutes after the show has finished the phone and computer lines run hot (or not, as the case may be).
In fact, I will always remember my first cooking segment on 'Healthy, Wealthy & Wise'. At a time when warm salads were still a bit of a novelty, I whipped up a simple warm chicken salad. And, boy, did those lines run hot (over 10 000 requests) with me, of course, patting myself on the back and thinking 'how easy is this'.

Fuelled by such success, what else could I do but get a little carried away, and the next week I presented a highly complicated restaurant-style dish. Needless to say, I was quickly brought back to earth, as the calls (to say the least) were conspicuous by their absence.

Fortunately, I am not completely stupid and it was quickly obvious that my place in the TV scheme of things was to encourage viewers to get off their butts, forget the supermarket freezer cabinet or local takeaway shop and get into that kitchen and whip up something simple.

And, at the risk of sounding big headed, it appears to have worked, because the recipe requests, except on the odd occasion when I can't help myself and get carried away, have continued to flood in.

I have also been frequently asked when I am going to put out a book featuring such dishes from my various shows. So, here then is that collection, which I hope will quickly become one of those dog-eared, food stained little numbers which are invariably found in the kitchen – right where they belong (rather than on the coffee table with those poncy designer efforts).

Asparagus, Broad Bean & Crispy Prosciutto Salad Tolarno's Crumbed Mushrooms • Soldiers of Parmesan Crumbed Fish with a Soft Boiled Egg • Thai Squid Salad • Barbecued Tomato, Onion & Fennel Salad Indian Spring Rolls • Crispy Wings with Garlic & Chilli • Almost a True Blue Greek Salad • Duck Livers with Balsamic & Chervil • Lamb's Brains in Mustard Crumbs with Spinach & Crispy Pancetta • Sweet Potato Curry Puffs • Roasted Tomato & Fetta Toast Leek & Ham Rolls • Polenta Chips • Watermelon & Fetta Salad • A Fresh, Tangy Moroccan Salad • Crostini alla Toscana • Smoked Trout Salad on Casalinga Bread Potato Cakes with Smoked Eel, Crispy Prosciutto & a Horseradish & Chive Sour Cream • Pizza Soufflé with Smoked Salmon

Hi
Hewy – Baby!
we love your show
& have your books
but my Mum wan

Great Beginnings

Sure, on the odd occasion that we invite the boss over for dinner, we do tend to pull out all the stops and whip up a starter to get the ball rolling. But, on most days, these dishes can also be thought of as light meal alternatives particularly if accompanied by a well-dressed green salad, or as part of a series of dishes served in the centre of the table (my favourite way of eating).

I also feel that even for a casual meal, a fresh tangy salad along with some hot crusty bread sets the scene rather well. And by the way, just in case you feel that I have got a bit carried away with the fetta cheese, it's my new 'fave', so there. (It also seems to be pretty popular with the hot restaurant chefs, so maybe I'm getting trendy in my old age.)

And, just one last thing, throughout the book there are many, many dishes such as pastas, seafood dishes and many of the vegetarian options which could so easily have been included in this section.

Asparagus, Broad Bean & Crispy Prosciutto Salad

SERVES 4

12 broad beans
table salt

Double peel by removing from pod and briefly blanching in plenty of lightly salted boiling water. Drain and squeeze to remove from shell. Set aside.

2 bunches of small asparagus, tips only

Add to boiling water, bring back to the boil and remove.

olive oil
8 slices prosciutto

At the same time, heat a little oil in a pan and fry prosciutto until crisp, then drain on paper towels.

$^1/_2$ head of garlic, roasted (see below)
$^1/_4$ cup extra virgin olive oil
a splash of soy sauce
$^1/_2$ tspn honey
juice of $^1/_2$ lemon

Squeeze garlic out of the husk and whisk up with the rest (adding as much or as little of the garlic as you like).

2 tbsp chopped chives
12 sprigs of Italian (flat leaf) parsley

Put in a bowl, add beans, asparagus, prosciutto and dressing, to taste.

'To roast a head of garlic, cut in half crossways, season, wrap in lightly oiled foil, and cook in a moderate 160°C oven for 15–20 minutes until soft and mellow.'

Tolarno's Crumbed Mushrooms

(SERVES 4)

6 cups vegetable oil	Heat in a fryer or wok to 190°C (see page 15).
30–40 baby button mushrooms	Wipe with a damp cloth.
plain flour breadcrumbs 2 eggs milk	Line up 3 bowls. Put flour in one, crumbs in the next and whisk eggs and 1 cup milk in the third. Then crumb mushrooms by dusting with flour, then dipping into egg wash before pressing firmly into crumbs. Deep-fry until golden. Then drain well on paper towels (don't overcrowd, do in 3 or 4 lots if necessary).
tartare sauce, bought or homemade (see page 75)	Serve on the side.

 'This is Tolarno's most popular starter – I reckon we have served about 4 million of the blessed things.
(To make things easier, a deep-frying thermometer is a worthwhile investment.)'

Soldiers of Parmesan Crumbed Fish with a Soft Boiled Egg

(SERVES 4)

1 cup breadcrumbs
$^1/_2$ cup freshly grated parmesan
1 tbsp chopped fresh parsley
plain flour
$^3/_4$ cup milk
1 large egg

Mix breadcrumbs, parmesan and parsley in one bowl. Put flour in another and whisk milk and egg together in a third.

400–500 g boneless firm fish fillets, skinned

Cut into even slices. Dust with flour, dip into egg wash and press firmly into crumbs. Set aside.

6 cups vegetable oil

Put in a wok and heat to 180°–190°C (see page 15).

4 large eggs
freshly ground salt

When oil is hot, put eggs in boiling water and, once they come back to the boil, cook for 5 minutes. At the same time, in 2 or 3 lots, cook fish until golden, drain well on paper towels and sprinkle with salt.

fresh tomato sauce, optional (see page 219)

To serve, put eggs in eggcups with tops cut off and put fish soldiers and a bowl of sauce alongside. To eat, dip fish into egg and then sauce.

'When I was a kid, one of my favourite treats was soldiers of toast with vegemite (crusts cut off and cut, lengthways, into 3 or 4), which I then dipped into my soft boiled egg — wonderful stuff.'

Dear Huey...

>It would be nice if you put out a book of your favourite recipes! I personally know lots of people who would buy it.
R Cotter

>I like your show. It is simple and direct. One point I have noticed. When scraping chopped-up food from chopping board to bowl, use the BACK of the knife or you will blunt the edge which you have spent some time sharpening.
Barry QLD

>I have just been watching your Cooking Adventures and I thought you would get a laugh out of a recipe I found in a camp oven cookbook I have: Camel Stew. You need 3 medium-sized camels, 1 ton salt, 1 ton pepper, 500 bushels potatoes, 200 bushels carrots, 3000 sprigs parsley, 2 small rabbits. It takes about 3 months to cut up and cook. It feeds 3800 people and if more are expected, add 2 rabbits.
Alison VIC

>Here is a limerick I wrote for you:
Huey's recipes are definitely yummy,
They are the perfect thing to fill my tummy.
They are easy to follow
And a delight to swallow.
Making them is a wise use of money!
Amy VIC

Thai Squid Salad

(SERVES 6–8)

4 tbsp water 3 chillies, finely sliced 1 garlic clove, crushed $1/4$ red onion, finely chopped 1 tbsp freshly grated ginger 1 tbsp Asian fish sauce 2 tbsp fresh lime juice 4 tbsp vegetable oil 2 spring (green) onions, sliced $1/2$ lemongrass stalk, finely sliced 2 tspn caster sugar	Put in a pot, bring to the boil and simmer for a few minutes.
6 baby squid, cleaned (see below), cut in half lengthways & scored in a diamond pattern with a sharp knife	Add to pot and simmer for 1 minute, stirring. Put into a bowl.
$1/2$ red onion, finely sliced 6 baby carrots, peeled & sliced $1/2$ avocado, diced 2 tbsp roasted peanuts $1/8$ continental (telegraph) cucumber, diced $1/2$ red capsicum, cored, seeded & diced 1 celery stalk, diced $1/2$ cup bean shoots coriander sprigs	Add, toss well and serve in a large bowl with sprigs of coriander scattered on the top.

'To clean squid, first of all separate head and tentacles from the body. Then cut tentacles off in a V shape just below the eyes and remove and discard the hard ball at the top. Clean skin and peel the flap and outside membrane from the tube. Then pull out the cartilage from the inside and wash and dry the lot.'

Barbecued Tomato, Onion & Fennel Salad

(SERVES 4)

olive oil
3 small fennel bulbs, halved & core removed
1–2 red onions, thickly sliced
freshly ground salt & pepper

Preheat grill or BBQ.
Toss vegies in a bowl with a little oil and seasonings. Then grill, brushing and regularly turning until lightly coloured.

3–4 tomatoes, cored & thickly sliced

Add tomatoes, brush with oil, season and cook for a few minutes, turning once.

extra virgin olive oil
balsamic vinegar
torn fresh basil leaves

Spoon vegies onto a platter in 3 separate piles, sprinkle with a little oil and balsamic and scatter basil leaves over the top.

'For a dish such as this where the fennel is only briefly cooked, I cut out the rather woody core in a V shape and discard.'

Indian Spring Rolls

(SERVES 8)

3 large potatoes, unpeeled but scrubbed	Cook until tender, then cool, peel and dice.
vegetable oil 1 medium onion, finely chopped 2 chillies, finely sliced 1 tspn freshly grated ginger	Heat a little oil in a wok and gently sauté vegies.
3 tbsp water 2 tbsp lemon juice 1 cup frozen peas 1 scant tspn garam masala 1 scant tspn ground coriander a pinch of cayenne freshly ground salt 3 tbsp chopped fresh coriander	Add and bring to the boil. Then add potatoes, turn off heat and mash coarsely. Cool.
flour bought puff pastry sheets	Lightly flour a work bench and cut pastry sheets into 4. Place teaspoons of mix in centre and paint outer edge with water. Roll up, folding edges in like an envelope and set aside.
6 cups vegetable oil	Heat oil in a wok or deep pot to 180°–190°C (see page 15) then fry until golden. Drain well on paper towels.

 'For the perfect accompaniment, whip up some raita by combining 1 cup yoghurt with chopped mint, a squeeze of lemon, a little grated cucumber and a pinch of cayenne.'

Crispy Wings with Garlic & Chilli

(SERVES 4)

16–20 chicken wings	Remove tips and cut in half at joint (set aside tips for a stock).
6 tbsp soy sauce 1 heaped tbsp honey 2 tbsp sherry 3 garlic cloves, crushed 1 tbsp sambal oelek freshly ground pepper	Whisk together and toss with wings. Refrigerate overnight.
4–6 cups vegetable oil cornflour	Heat oil in a wok to 180°–190°C (see page 15). Toss wings in cornflour and in 2 or 3 lots, deep-fry until golden. Drain well on paper towels.
finely chopped chillies finely chopped spring (green) onion lime wedges	Sprinkle with chilli and onion and serve with lime wedges.

'This also works brilliantly with quails that have either been semi-boned (leaving wings and leg bones in) or with the back bone cut out and squashed reasonably flat with the palm of the hand.'

Almost a True Blue Greek Salad

(SERVES 4)

$^1/_2$ cup fresh herb leaves (oregano, thyme,
   mint & basil)
$^1/_2$ cup olive oil
juice of $^1/_2$ lemon
1 garlic clove
freshly ground salt & pepper

Whiz up in a blender.

1 red onion, finely sliced
a handful of frisee lettuce
150 g fetta cheese, cubed
12–18 pitted black olives, sliced
$^1/_2$ continental (telegraph) cucumber sliced
   & halved
12 cherry tomatoes, halved

Gently toss in a large bowl. Then toss again
with dressing to taste.

'This salad always invokes memories of wonderful sunny days in the Greek
Isles eating spotlessly fresh fish (from the boats moored just metres away)
lots of freshly made bread and copious quantities of pretty ordinary wine
(in fairness it was quite a long time ago).'

Duck Livers with Balsamic & Chervil

(SERVES 4)

olive oil
16 duck livers, cleaned
freshly ground salt & pepper

Heat a little oil in a large pan and, in 2 lots, seal livers on both sides. Remove to a plate and season.

1 large onion, sliced

Add a little more oil, if necessary, and gently cook onion until golden brown.

4 tbsp balsamic vinegar
fresh chervil sprigs

Add balsamic and bubble for a few seconds. Then return livers and any juices to pan and cook until pink in the centre. Toss in some chervil sprigs.

4 thick slices country-style bread, grilled
  or toasted
extra virgin olive oil

Put bread on plates, top with liver mix and sprinkle with oil.

'Of course you could use any poultry livers (or, in fact, lamb's fry or calf's liver too).'

Lamb's Brains in Mustard Crumbs with Spinach & Crispy Pancetta

(SERVES 4)

4–6 sets of brains
$1/2$ lemon juice
1 parsley sprig
$1/4$ onion, sliced
a splash of white vinegar
water

Soak brains for a few hours in cold water with a squeeze of lemon. Drain and put in a pot with parsley, onion, vinegar and water to cover. Bring to the boil, turn off and allow to cool in the water. Then drain well and separate into two, removing any membranes.

Dijon mustard
breadcrumbs

Brush generously with mustard and press firmly into crumbs.

olive oil
a knob of butter

Heat in a pan and gently fry brains until golden brown (turn very carefully). Remove and keep warm.

8 slices pancetta

Add a little more oil to pan, if necessary, and fry until crisp. Drain well.

a large handful of baby spinach, well washed
extra virgin olive oil
balsamic vinegar

Put a mound of spinach on each plate and dress with oil and vinegar. Top with pancetta and then brains.

'It is essential that the brains are soaked in acidulated water before cooking to get rid of any blood.'

Sweet Potato Curry Puffs

(SERVES 4–8)

vegetable oil

1 tbsp curry powder

$^1/_2$ tspn paprika

6 curry leaves

Heat a little oil in a pot. Mix curry powder and paprika with a little water to form a paste and then fry with the curry leaves until it begins to sizzle.

1 medium carrot, peeled & finely diced

1 large onion, finely chopped

1 large sweet potato, peeled & finely diced

Add and toss for a few minutes, scraping bottom of pot with a wooden spoon.

$^3/_4$ cup water

a pinch of sugar

freshly ground salt

Add, turn heat down and cook, very gently, until vegies are tender (about 12–15 minutes). Mash and cool.

bought puff pastry sheets

With 8 cm pastry cutter cut rounds, put small spoonfuls of filling in centre, moisten edge with cold water and fold over. Then crimp edge with a fork to seal.

6 cups vegetable oil

Heat to 180°–190°C (see page 15) in a wok or deep sided pot and deep-fry until puffed and golden (don't overcrowd). Drain well on paper towels.

'If you don't have a deep-frying thermometer, just throw in a cube of bread to check temperature. If it sinks to the bottom it is not hot enough, and if it burns it is too hot. But if it sizzles gently and turns golden around the edges in a minute or so you are ready for action.'

Roasted Tomato & Fetta Toast

(SERVES 4)

8–12 extra large cherry tomatoes olive oil freshly ground salt & pepper	Preheat oven to 180°C. Put tomatoes in a baking dish and sprinkle with oil and seasonings. Roast until they begin to collapse.
1 tbsp chopped fresh basil, 4 tbsp olive oil	While tomatoes are cooking, combine and set aside.
4 thick slices country-style bread 1 garlic clove, cut in half	When tomatoes are ready, toast or grill bread and rub vigorously with cut side of garlic.
100 g fetta cheese balsamic vinegar	Place toast on plates, top with tomatoes and crumble fetta over the top. Then sprinkle with basil oil and a little balsamic.

'I am often accused of having a bit of an addiction to garlic, but compared to famed Chez Panisse restaurateur, Alice Waters, I am an amateur. For her annual garlic festival, she features a degustation menu of many courses each of which (including dessert) features copious quantities of the blessed stuff.'

Leek & Ham Rolls

(SERVES 4–6)

6 medium leeks
table salt

Preheat oven to 220°C.
Remove outer and damaged leaves, wash well and cut into 2 crossways. Cook in lightly salted water until crisp-tender. Drain well.

12 slices ham
mornay sauce (see page 86)
grated tasty cheese

Wrap leeks in ham and put in an oven dish with seam down. Then top with a generous amount of mornay and then grated cheese. Cook in oven for about 10 minutes until golden and bubbling.

Serve as a starter or as a light lunch with a tangy green salad on the side.

'It seemed a terrific idea at the time. We were in Noosa filming, the rain had finally stopped and the bench was set up on the footpath in Hastings Street. Then just as I was finishing the recipe, a car came speeding through the rather large puddle and, you guessed it, drenched the lot of us. Needless to say we retired for the day and went to Soleil for lunch instead.'

Polenta Chips

(SERVES 4)

2 garlic cloves
a little chicken stock

Cook garlic in stock until tender and set aside.

250 g polenta
500 ml cold water

Combine.

500 ml cold water
a little salt

Bring to the boil in a large pot. Then add polenta mix and cook for 5 minutes, stirring vigorously. Then turn heat down to low and cook for about 30 minutes until mixture comes away from sides of pot.

100 g freshly grated parmesan
vegetable oil

Drain and chop garlic and then add to polenta with cheese. Put into an oiled baking tray and spread out to about $1^1/_2$ cm thick. Cool overnight.

breadcrumbs
2 eggs
$^1/_2$ cup milk
plain flour

Cut into about 8 x $1^1/_2$ cm chips and crumb (see page 4).

6 cups vegetable oil
sweet chilli sauce , optional

Heat oil to 190°C (see page 15) in a wok or deep pot and deep-fry polenta chips until golden brown. Drain well and serve with sauce on the side.

'Another Tolarno classic, this was featured in my first book **A Cook's Journey**. But we have had so many requests for the recipe, I felt I should repeat it (particularly because A Cook's Journey is out of print).'

Watermelon & Fetta Salad

(SERVES 4)

$^1/_4$ cup extra virgin olive oil
1$^1/_2$ tbsp fresh lemon juice
$^1/_2$ tspn harissa, bought or homemade
   (see page 185)
freshly ground salt & pepper

Whisk.

4 cups watermelon, seeded & cubed
$^1/_2$ small red onion, finely sliced
100 g feta cheese, crumbled
10 pitted black olives, sliced
12 Italian (flat leaf) parsley sprigs
12 fresh mint leaves, torn

Gently toss with dressing to taste.

'This sounds a little weird but is actually rather delicious. And, when buying fetta, look for a cheese that is roughish around the edges (a bit like me) and crumbly, rather than those smooth versions which are often tasteless.'

A Fresh, Tangy Moroccan Salad

(SERVES 4)

6 large ripe tomatoes, peeled, seeded & diced (see page 206)	Toss together.
2 celery stalks, diced	
1 green capsicum, cored, seeded & diced	
a small handful of frisee lettuce	
1 tbsp chopped fresh parsley	
1 tbsp chopped fresh mint	
1 tbsp chopped fresh coriander	
2 pieces preserved lemon, finely sliced (see page 226)	
10 pitted green olives, sliced	
extra virgin olive oil	Toss through to taste.
balsamic vinegar	
freshly ground salt & pepper	
½ cup yoghurt	Mix together and sprinkle over the salad
2 tbsp chopped fresh coriander	(serving any left over on the side).
1 heaped tspn harissa, bought or homemade (see page 185)	
a squeeze of fresh lemon juice	
8 slices flat bread	Heat in an unoiled non-stick pan or on a grill (or wrap in foil and heat in the oven) and serve on the side.

'This salad can also be used as an accompaniment – in which case, forget the flat bread.'

Crostini alla Toscana

(SERVES 4–6)

olive oil $\frac{1}{2}$ onion, finely chopped 1 garlic clove, crushed	Heat a little oil in a pan and sauté for a few minutes.
12–15 chicken livers, cleaned freshly ground salt & pepper	Add and toss until sealed.
3 tbsp muscat or tokay	Add, turn heat down and gently simmer for 5 minutes. Remove from heat and crush with a fork.
4–6 thickish slices of French bread fresh thyme sprigs	Toast or grill bread, heap with liver mix and garnish with thyme.

'I am always fascinated by people who tell me they will not eat offal but then happily eat a dish such as this or liver pâté. What do they actually think is the prime ingredient (or is it just a case of out of sight, out of mind)?'

Smoked Trout Salad on Casalinga Bread

(SERVES 2–4)

1 tbsp chopped fresh dill 4 tbsp mayonnaise, bought or homemade (see below) 1^1/$_2$ tbsp sour cream 1 heaped tspn Dijon mustard a squeeze of fresh lemon juice	Mix together.
1 smoked trout fillet, flaked 1 celery stalk, diced 1 spring (green) onion chopped	Add and gently mix through.
2–4 thick slices casalinga or any country- style bread	Grill or toast
2–4 sprigs fresh dill	Mound bread with salad and garnish with sprig of dill.

'To make homemade mayonnaise, just throw 2 eggs, 2 yolks, 1 tablespoon mustard and a pinch of salt into the food processor. Whiz up for one minute, then add 500 ml of any good oil, little by little, through the feeder tube. When all the oil is added, flavour to taste with fresh lemon juice and seasonings.'

Potato Cakes with Smoked Eel, Crispy Prosciutto & a Horseradish & Chive Sour Cream

(SERVES 4)

4–6 large potatoes, peeled & cubed table salt	Cook in boiling, salted water until tender. Drain very well.
olive oil freshly ground salt & pepper 2 heaped tbsp mayonnaise 2 spring (green) onions, finely chopped	Mash with a splash of oil and then mix in the rest. Form into 4 patties using a pastry cutter (or just your hands).
plain flour olive oil	Lightly flour patties and fry in moderately hot oil in a large non-stick pan. Then cook until golden brown on both sides and drain well.
4 heaped tbsp sour cream 1 tbsp creamed horseradish 1 tbsp snipped fresh chives	While patties are cooking mix together.
2 fillets smoked eel, halved 4–8 slices of prosciutto, fried until crisp in a little olive oil	To serve, place a patty on each plate, top with horseradish sour cream, the eel and a slice or two of prosciutto.

'I love smoked eel but will admit it's a bit of an acquired taste. So if you haven't as yet acquired that taste, use smoked trout or salmon instead.'

Pizza Soufflé with Smoked Salmon

(SERVES 4)

20 g fresh yeast lukewarm water	Mix yeast with a little water until dissolved.
500 g strong bread flour	Place in a bowl, make a well in centre and pour in yeast. Mix with a wooden spoon, adding lukewarm water little by little until a fairly soft dough is formed. Then, with your hands, knead until dough comes away from bowl adding a little more flour if necessary.
olive oil	Lightly oil a bowl, put in dough, cover with a clean tea towel and leave in a warm spot for about 1 hour until doubled in size. Turn out onto a floured surface, roll out and, with a pastry cutter, cut into 6–8 cm Rounds. Put a layer of oil in pan, heat and fry pizza until risen and golden. Drain well.
sliced smoked salmon sour cream snipped fresh chives	Top with salmon, sour cream and chives.

'The idea for this fried pizza comes from Antonio Carluccio who, along with Keith Floyd, is my favourite TV chef.

Cock-A-Leekie Soup • Old-Fashioned Chicken & Sweetcorn Soup • Corn Soup with Capsicum & Coriander •

Four Soups in One • Bread & Tomato Soup with Pesto & a Poached Egg  West Indian Sweet

Potato Soup  Chicken Enchilada Soup • Blue Eye & Smoked Oyster Chowder • Italian

Cabbage & Sausage Soup • Green Onion Soup with Whipped Potato • Roasted Vegetable 'Minestrone' with

Pesto  Grandma Hewitson's Ham Hock Soup

Hi
Hewy - Baby!
We love your show
& have your books
but my mum wan

Super Soups

'A home is a place where a pot of fresh soup simmers gently on the stove, filling the kitchen with soft aromas – and filling your heart and, later your tummy, with joy.'

Keith Floyd

For a while there it seemed that soups had gone out of fashion. The stalwart of my mother's kitchen, soups were always regarded as filling (an important factor when dealing with growing boys), easy to make and, above all, the perfect way to use whatever was going wild in Dad's garden.

Of course, these days, many of us don't have the luxury of a vegie garden (or the space to put one in) but the bargains at our markets, super or otherwise, are not to be ignored. Because with just a few spuds and an onion or two you can whip up a hearty little number. And by adding half a pumpkin or a few ears of sweetcorn you are suddenly talking posh. So give it a go. Get out the stockpot and get back into the habit of producing hearty flavour-filled soups just like our mums and grandmums used to make.

And, who knows? Maybe then all the tummies in your household really will be filled with joy.

Cock-A-Leekie Soup

(SERVES 6–8)

4–6 large chicken thighs with bone,
skin removed
2 litres chicken stock, bought or homemade
(see page 62)
2–3 medium leeks, well washed & sliced
1 medium carrot, diced
2 celery stalks, diced
1 garlic clove, crushed
a few parsley sprigs
2 bay leaves
a few thyme sprigs
freshly ground salt & pepper

Put in a pot and gently simmer for about 25 minutes. Remove chicken, bay leaves and herb sprigs. When chicken is cool enough to handle, remove meat from bone and shred.

$3/4$ cup basmati rice
1 tbsp chopped fresh parsley

Add to pot along with chicken meat and simmer gently until rice is tender.

'Cock-a-Leekie is a traditional Scottish soup dating back to the sixteenth century.'

Old-Fashioned Chicken & Sweetcorn Soup

(SERVES 4)

150 g skinless chicken breast	Chop chicken until finely minced. Then place in a bowl, add cornflour and soy. Mix well.
2 tspn cornflour	
2 tspn soy sauce	
1 tbsp vegetable oil	Heat oil in a pot and seal chicken, stirring continually.
320 g canned creamed sweetcorn	Add and simmer for 10 minutes.
2 cups cold water	
freshly ground salt & pepper	
1 tspn cornflour	Combine and add to soup, stirring continually.
2 tbsp cold water	
1 egg, whisked	Remove from heat and stir in egg. Then check seasoning and add a splash of soy and spring onion.
soy sauce	
1–2 spring (green) onions, sliced	

'The last time I ordered this classic in an Asian restaurant would be, at the very least, circa 1970. So, when a viewer asked for the recipe, I was pleasantly surprised when I discovered how delicious it is.'

Corn Soup with Capsicum & Coriander

(SERVES 4–6)

olive oil
1 large onion, chopped
2 garlic cloves, crushed
a pinch of cayenne

Heat a little oil in a large pot and sauté until vegies are soft.

1 red capsicum, cored, seeded & diced
1 green capsicum, cored, seeded & diced
6–8 large corn cobs

Add capsicum and then, with a sharp knife, cut kernels from cobs and add. Toss well.

6 cups vegetable stock, bought or homemade (see page 198)
freshly ground salt & pepper

Add along with 3 of the stripped corncobs. Boil, vigorously, for 10 minutes. Remove corncobs & discard.

handful coarsely chopped fresh coriander

Add, check seasoning and then blend half. Return to pot, stir well and check seasoning.

'By blending only half you get a more rustic, peasant-style soup.'

Four Soups in One

(SERVES 6–8)

1. POTATO, LEEK & ONION SOUP

3 large potatoes, peeled & chopped
4 large onions, peeled & chopped
4 medium leeks, well washed & chopped
chicken or vegetable stock, bought or
    homemade (see page 62 or 198)
freshly ground salt & pepper

Put vegies in a large pot, cover well with
stock and simmer until tender.

a good slurp of cream

Add, blend and check seasoning.

2. VICHYSSOISE

Potato, Leek & Onion Soup (see above)
extra salt
extra cream

When blending, add extra cream and
seasoning and chill at least overnight.
(When chilled, the salt tends to fade.)

snipped chives

Garnish with chives.

'This was another of our very popular **Healthy, Wealthy & Wise** recipes.
I got myself into a bit of trouble doing all the soups at once – I had
microwaves turning, blenders whizzing, pots bubbling and even the
freezer working overtime (chilling the vichyssoise). But eventually it came
together and, luckily for me, I ended up with 4 different bowls of delicious
soup (with, I must admit, enough left over to feed a small army).'

3. PUMPKIN SOUP

Potato, Leek and Onion Soup (see page 32)
1 butternut pumpkin

Microwave whole pumpkin on high for 15 minutes or until skin peels off easily. Then peel, remove seeds and chop coarsely.

a large knob of unsalted butter
extra cream
freshly ground salt & pepper

Blend pumpkin and potato soup with butter and extra cream. Check seasoning.

4. LETTUCE SOUP WITH MINTED SOUR CREAM

Potato, Leek & Onion Soup (see page 32, unblended)
1 large iceberg lettuce, core and damaged outer leaves removed
freshly ground salt & pepper

Bring potato soup mix to the boil. Slice lettuce and add. The minute it comes back to the boil, remove from heat and blend. (This preserves the colour.) Season to taste.

$^{1}/_{2}$ cup sour cream
2 tbsp chopped fresh fresh mint

Combine and serve a dollop on top.

FURTHER THOUGHTS
on Four Soups in One

★ Whip up a red capsicum version by coring and seeding 4 or 5 large red capsicum and throwing them into the pot along with 2 crushed garlic cloves. When soft, whiz up and add a little red wine vinegar to taste.

★ Instead of the lettuce, add some podded green peas (or, dare I say, frozen minted ones). And, in a similar fashion, the second the soup comes back to the boil whip it off and blend. (For an extra bit of zing, try adding a splash of champers at the table.)

★ Carrot soup is surprisingly delicious but it was always a bit of a failure in my restaurants until I changed its name to Crème Crecy (its rather posh French name). It then walked out the door. So maybe, to stop the kids turning their noses up at home, call it Crecy Soup (which, I promise you, will soon become Crazy Soup and no one will ever remember why) and make it by throwing some chopped, peeled carrots into the base and after blending throw in a generous knob of butter and some freshly chopped parsley.

★ Give the pumpkin version a bit of a kick by throwing in a couple of tablespoons of good curry powder or paste along with the chopped pumpkin.

★ Experiment with garnishes by adding different herbs or spices to sour cream, yoghurt or even plain old whipped cream.

★ Try two soups in one bowl. For example fill the bowl two thirds with the pumpkin soup and then, in the centre, add some capsicum soup — it's a bit of fun and tastes good too.

Bread & Tomato Soup with Pesto & a Poached Egg

(SERVES 4)

olive oil	Heat a little oil in a heavy-bottomed
1 large onion, finely sliced	pot and sauté until soft.
2 garlic cloves, crushed	
800 g canned diced tomatoes, drained a little	Add and boil for 10–15 minutes.
4 cups chicken stock, bought or homemade (see page 62)	
freshly ground salt & pepper	
3 anchovies, mashed	
$^1/_4$ loaf country-style bread, crusts removed & cubed	Add and cook for 3–4 minutes. Check seasoning.
4 large eggs, poached	Top each bowl with pesto and a
pesto, bought or homemade (see page 42)	poached egg.

'Although most saucepans these days are made from stainless steel, do remember that ingredients such as tomatoes, which are high in acid, must be cooked in same. Because if cooked in aluminium or cast iron, the soup could quite possibly turn a very unappetising black and have an unpleasant taste to boot.'

West Indian Sweet Potato Soup

(SERVES 6–8)

vegetable oil 2 celery stalks, diced 2 medium carrots, peeled & diced 1 large onion, chopped	Heat oil in a large pot and sauté for 5 minutes.
1 tbsp Indian curry paste 4 chillies, chopped 4 garlic cloves, crushed	Add and cook for another minute or so.
4–6 sweet potatoes, peeled & chopped 2 bay leaves 4 fresh thyme sprigs vegetable stock, bought or homemade (see page 198)	Add along with stock to cover. Simmer until vegies are tender. Blend.
yoghurt	Garnish with a dollop of yoghurt.

 'The sweet potato, which is not actually a potato, is thought to have originated in Peru before being brought to Hawaii and hence to New Zealand in the 13th Century. (As proof of this rather bold statement, may I point out that the sweet potato's Peruvian name, kumar, is remarkably similar to the Maori name – kumara.)'

Chicken Enchilada Soup

(SERVES 6–8)

olive oil
1 large onion, chopped
2 garlic cloves, crushed
2 chillies, chopped

Heat a little oil in a large pot and sauté vegies until soft.

1 tbsp sambal oelek
$1/2$ tspn cumin
$1/2$ tspn ground coriander

Add and stir for a minute or two.

6 cups chicken stock, bought or homemade
  (see page 62)
2 skinless chicken breasts, finely diced
2 corn cobs, kernels removed
a good splash of soy sauce
2 tbsp chopped fresh parsley

Add and bring to the simmer. Then gently cook for 20–30 minutes.

2 cups grated tasty cheese
4 large flour tortillas, sliced

Add, turn heat up and cook for 5 minutes, adding more stock if necessary.

Tabasco
freshly ground salt & pepper

Season to taste with salt, pepper and Tabasco.

'Hardly an authentic little Mexican number, but delicious none the less.'

Blue Eye & Smoked Oyster Chowder

(SERVES 4–6)

olive oil

1 large onion, chopped

2 celery stalks, diced

1 medium carrot, diced

1 leek, sliced

Heat a little oil in a large heavy-bottomed pot and sauté vegies until soft.

6 cups fish or vegetable stock, bought or homemade (see page 94 or 198)

kernels from 3 corn cobs

8 baby potatoes, scrubbed & quartered

Add along with stripped corn cobs and cook for about 15 minutes until potatoes are tender.

300 g blue eye (or any firm, steaky fish), cubed

1–2 cans smoked oysters, drained

$^1/_4$ cup cream

2 tbsp chopped fresh parsley

Remove corn cobs, add and simmer gently for a few minutes.

'This is a recipe which I pinched from a restaurant in Boston. Boston which is, of course, famous for its clam chowder is also a city with the most wonderful oyster bars (which sell little apart from chowder and freshly shucked oysters). But their barmen do get a little carried away. Because in every single one we were pointed out the very chair in which famous Bostonian John F. Kennedy sat most days. (I'm surprised he had time to become President of the United States.)'

Italian Cabbage & Sausage Soup

(SERVES 6–8)

olive oil 2 garlic cloves crushed 2 medium onions, chopped	Heat a little oil in a large pot and sauté until softish.
4 Italian sausages	Skin, add to pot and seal, mashing with a wooden spoon as you do so.
$^{1}/_{2}$–1 small savoy cabbage, sliced, core and ribs removed 8 cups chicken stock, bought or homemade (see page 62) freshly ground salt & pepper	Add and boil for 45 minutes, stirring regularly.
1 cup risotto rice 3–4 tbsp pesto, bought or homemade (see page 42)	Add, mix in well and cook for 15–20 minutes until rice is tender.
freshly grated parmesan	Serve with parmesan on the side.

'I think I may have mentioned this before, but my mother always said that if you could stand a spoon up in a soup it was more of a meal than a soup – this is such a number.'

Green Onion Soup with Whipped Potato

(SERVES 6–8)

6 large onions, chopped
10 spring (green) onions, cleaned and
    coarsely chopped
3 leeks, well washed & chopped
freshly ground salt & pepper
chicken or vegetable stock, bought or
    homemade (see page 62 or 198)

Put vegies in a large pot, season and cover with stock. Cook until very tender and then blend.

3 large potatoes, peeled & chopped
$^1/_2$ tspn table salt
1 garlic clove, crushed

At the same time boil potatoes in water with salt and garlic until very tender.

a good splash of cream
a little hot milk
balsamic vinegar

Then mash potatoes, along with cream and milk until very smooth. Put a mound in the centre of each soup bowl and pour the hot soup around. Sprinkle with a little balsamic.

'Scoop up a little of the potato and then fill the spoon with soup – delicious.'

Roasted Vegetable 'Minestrone' with Pesto

(SERVES 4)

15 basil leaves
1 garlic clove
2 tbsp grated parmesan
olive oil
freshly ground salt & pepper

Make pesto by whizzing up in a blender or processor with enough olive oil to make a thinnish paste.

olive oil
2 red onions, peeled & cut in wedges
2 medium carrots, peeled & sliced on the diagonal
3 celery stalks, sliced on the diagonal
1 red capsicum, cored, seeded & cut in strips
1 green capsicum, cored, seeded & cut in strips
2 Japanese eggplant, sliced & halved

Preheat oven to 200°C.
Put in a roasting tray, drizzle with oil, season generously and roast for 20 minutes.

500 g cherry tomatoes

Add, toss and cook for another 10 minutes.

6–8 cups vegetable stock, bought or homemade (see page 198), well seasoned

Heat stock. Put vegies in bowls and pour stock over the top.

parmesan shavings

Sprinkle with pesto and parmesan.

 'Vary the vegies depending on the season.'

Grandma Hewitson's Ham Hock Soup

(FOR 6–8)

2 cups dried soup mix

Soak overnight in cold water and then drain.

1 large carrot, peeled & diced
1 large potato, peeled & diced
1 turnip, peeled & diced
1 large onion, peeled & diced
1 medium leek, well washed & sliced
2 garlic cloves, crushed
2 tspn dried oregano
2 tspn dried thyme
2 tspn paprika
2 smoked ham hocks
1 cup dry white wine
6 cups chicken stock, bought or homemade
   (see page 62)
freshly ground salt

Put in the pressure cooker along with soup mix. Bring to pressure as per instructions and cook for 30 minutes. Remove hocks.

$1/4$ savoy cabbage, sliced, core & ribs removed
2 tbsp chopped fresh parsley

When cool enough to handle, skin the hocks, chop up meat and return to pot along with cabbage and parsley. Simmer for 10 minutes.

'My grandmother, who brought up a family of invariably hungry coal miners on soups such as these, often used bacon bones instead of the ham hocks, particularly when close to pay day.'

Braised Chicken with Morels & Vermouth Sauce • Chicken Parmigiana • Szechuan Chicken

Hungarian Chicken Ragout Claypot Chicken & Rice • Chicken Caesar Sandwich • Red Duck

Curry • Teriyaki Chicken with Grilled Pineapple • Glazed Roast Chicken with Orange, Honey & Hoisin •

Baby Chickens on Roasted Parsnips A Quick Sauté of Chicken • Chicken Pie with a Potato

Crust • Peking Duck Wraps • Chicken Stock • Oven-Fried Lemon Chicken Roulade of

Stuffed Chicken with Coriander & Lime Mayo • Lemony Turkey Rissoles • The Original Warm Chicken Salad

• Vietnamese Ginger & Lemongrass Chicken Spicy Mandarin Chicken Drumsticks

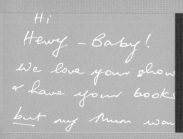

Hi
Hewy - Baby!
We love your show
& have your books
but my mum wan

Birds of a Feather

About the most requested recipes have involved chicken in one form or other. Of course we have whipped up the odd duck, quail and even, on one auspicious occasion, a pheasant (a notable success with the recipe request gaining a perfect 0).

So, being the culinary genius that I am, it was pretty obvious that chicken is one of today's foremost staples. Which is pretty understandable, because not only are today's birds almost invariably tender but they are sold in cook-friendly sizes and shapes, are freely available and are, to boot, pretty damned cheap. And while they may not quite have the flavour of yesteryear (except for some of the free-range varieties which are certainly not cheap) this can be easily fixed by thinking marinades, robust sauces or maybe even interesting garnishes which are guaranteed to add something special with little or no extra effort.

Braised Chicken with Morels & Vermouth Sauce

(SERVES 4)

olive oil	Heat oil in a pan. Flour chicken and brown.
8 chicken thighs, boned	Then remove from pan and discard oil.
plain flour	
a knob of butter	Add a little more oil with butter and heat.
1 large onion, chopped	Sauté onion until soft. Add morels and
8–12 morels, wiped clean & halved	garlic and cook for 1 minute more.
lengthways	
1 garlic clove, crushed	
$^1/_2$ cup dry vermouth	Add and bring to the boil. Then return
$1^1/_2$ cups chicken stock, bought or homemade	chicken, cover and cook very gently for
(see page 62)	about 20 minutes, turning chicken over a
1 tbsp chopped fresh parsley	couple of times and basting regularly.
freshly ground salt & pepper	Remove chicken when cooked.
cream	Add a little cream, bring back to boil and
	pour over chicken.

'Morels are in season for about 5 minutes so grab them while you can. But, at other times of the year, use field mushrooms, which I normally leave in the paper bag for a few days to accentuate their earthy flavour.'

Chicken Parmigiana

(SERVES 4)

olive oil
1 large onion, chopped
1 red capsicum, cored, seeded & diced
2 garlic cloves, crushed
$^{1}/_{4}$ cup chicken stock
800–1200 g canned diced tomatoes
6 basil leaves, sliced

Preheat oven to 200°C.
Heat a little oil in a pot and sauté onion, capsicum & garlic until softish. Then add stock and tomatoes and gently cook for 10 minutes. Mix in basil and set aside.

1 cup breadcrumbs
$^{1}/_{2}$ cup chopped fresh parsley
1 garlic clove, crushed

Mix together in a bowl.

1 cup milk
1 large egg
plain flour
4 skinless chicken breasts

Beat together egg and milk. Then lightly flour chicken before dipping into milk mix and finally into crumbs.

olive oil

Lightly cover base of a pan with oil, then heat. Fry chicken on both sides until golden brown.

grated mozzarella cheese
Green Bean Salad with Pesto, optional
   (see page 237).

Spread half the sauce in a baking dish, top with chicken, the rest of the sauce and a generous sprinkling of cheese. Bake for 12–15 minutes until bubbling. Serve with salad.

'Obviously a classic – I got so may requests for parmigiana that I felt that I had to have a shot. And although it was a bit of a Huey version, the true blue taste test worked – the crew polished it off in about 5 seconds flat.'

Szechuan Chicken

(SERVES 4)

2 skinless chicken breasts, cubed 1 egg white 2 tspn cornflour	Toss together, cover and refrigerate for 3 hours.
2 tbsp light soy sauce 2 tbsp chicken stock, bought or homemade (see page 62) a good pinch of sugar $\frac{1}{2}$ tspn grated fresh ginger 2 tspn white vinegar 1 tspn sambal oelek 1 garlic clove, crushed 2 chillies, sliced 2 tspn cornflour	Whisk together in a bowl.
vegetable oil 18 or so unsalted cashews	Heat a little oil in a wok and cook cashews until golden. Remove with a slotted spoon. Then toss chicken in and stir until it's sealed. Add sauce and simmer, adding more stock if necessary.
4 spring (green) onions, cut in 3 cm lengths	Add along with cashews and toss to heat.
steamed rice	Serve with rice.

 'The process of marinating the chicken in egg white and cornflour is called velveting. It tenderises the chook dramatically and is the secret behind the tender, juicy chicken strips to be found in every Asian restaurant stirfry.'

Hungarian Chicken Ragout

(SERVES 4)

olive oil
8 chicken thighs, boned

Heat oil in a pan and brown chicken. Remove.

2 medium onions, chopped
2 green capsicum, cored, seeded & diced

Add more oil if necessary and gently cook onion until lightly browned. Then add capsicum and cook for a few minutes more.

2 tbsp paprika
800 g canned diced tomatoes, drained a little
1½ cups chicken stock, bought or homemade
   (see page 62)
freshly ground salt

Add paprika and cook for 1 minute. Then add rest, mix well and bring to the boil. Return chicken and gently simmer for 15–20 minutes until chicken is cooked. Remove chicken.

½ cup sour cream
1 tbsp plain flour
1 tbsp chopped fresh parsley

Whisk together. Remove pan from heat and whisk into sauce.

chopped fresh parsley
Lemon Rice, optional (see page 233)

To serve, mound rice on plates, top with chicken, spoon over sauce and garnish with parsley.

 'I must have a death wish – because every time I attempt a Hungarian dish (which I'm the first to admit are not terribly authentic) I get what can only be deemed to be 'hate mail' from Hungarians who are irate at my bastardising their cuisine. But, interestingly, as I have mentioned before, each and every one of their so called 'truly authentic' versions invariably differs greatly.'

Claypot Chicken & Rice

(SERVES 4)

vegetable oil
1 onion, finely chopped
2 garlic cloves, crushed
1 heaped tspn grated ginger

Heat a little oil in a wok and sauté for a few minutes. Turn off heat.

2 tbsp soy sauce
2 tbsp oyster sauce
2 tbsp dry sherry
1 tbsp cornflour
1 tbsp Kecap Manis

Add and whisk well.

8 chicken thighs, boned

Cut in half lengthways. Pour above mix over and marinate for 30–60 minutes.

2 cups jasmine rice
3 cups chicken stock, bought or homemade (see page 62)

Preheat oven to 180°C.
Mix chicken and marinade with rice and put in a claypot. Pour stock over the top, cover and cook for 30 minutes, mixing once or twice.

spring (green) onion, sliced

Garnish with spring onion.

'I like to serve this as is, in the claypot.'

Chicken Caesar Sandwich

(SERVES 4)

$^1/_2$ cup mayonnaise, bought or homemade
   (see page 23)
3 anchovies, mashed
2 tbsp sour cream
1 tbsp hot water

Mix together.

2 skinless chicken breasts
olive oil
$^1/_2$ lemon
freshly ground salt & pepper

Flatten chicken out to an even thickness
with a meat mallet. Then brush with oil,
season and either grill or panfry with a
good squeeze of lemon juice.

4 rindless bacon rashers

When chicken is almost ready, grill or fry
until crisp.

8 thick slices country-style bread
1 garlic clove, halved

Toast or grill, then rub each slice vigorously
with the cut side of garlic.

cos lettuce leaves, well washed
shavings of parmesan

Smear 4 slices of bread with mayonnaise
and top with lettuce, bacon, sliced chicken
and parmesan. Top with other slices of
bread (also smeared with mayonnaise)
cut in half and serve.

'I sometimes poach an egg for each sandwich and place one on top of the chicken.
This makes the sangas particularly messy, but they are even more delicious.'

Red Duck Curry

(SERVES 4)

vegetable oil
1 chilli, finely sliced
1 garlic clove, sliced
½ lemongrass stalk, sliced
1 heaped tspn grated ginger

Preheat oven to highest degree.
Heat a little oil in a wok and sauté for
2–3 minutes.

1 heaped tbsp red curry paste
400 ml canned coconut cream
1–2 pinches white sugar
1 tbsp Asian fish sauce
2 kaffir lime leaves
2 Japanese (baby) eggplants, cut in thickish
   slices and halved
12 baby green beans, topped, tailed & halved
   crossways

Add, mix in well and gently simmer for
10 minutes.

vegetable oil
2–3 large duck breasts
1 small can straw mushrooms, drained
rice, to serve

At the same time, heat oil in an oven-proof
pan. Over high heat sear duck (skin side
down) for a few minutes. Then turn over
and put in the oven until firmish when
pressed (about 7–8 minutes). Remove and
set aside for a few minutes. Then cut in
thick slices and toss through sauce along
with mushrooms. Serve with rice.

'I find the odour of fish sauce (which may also be labelled nampla, nuoc
mam, nuoc nam or patis) particularly unappealing. But, interestingly, when
added to a sauce, that odour appears to dissipate and the sauce adds a
degree of extra oomph. And, for your information, fish sauce is made from
salted and fermented dried fish or prawns which are allowed to ferment in
wooden barrels for about 3 months – sounds appetising doesn't it?'

Teriyaki Chicken with Grilled Pineapple

(SERVES 4)

$^1/_2$ cup soy sauce

$^1/_4$ cup mirin (Japanese rice wine)

$^1/_4$ cup sake

$^1/_2$ tspn sesame oil

1 tbsp sugar

2 tspn freshly grated ginger

1 garlic clove, crushed

Whisk together.

4 skinless chicken breasts

Flatten out to an even thickness with a meat mallet, pour mix over and marinate overnight.

4–8 thick ring slices of fresh pineapple

Preheat BBQ or ridged grill.
Cook chicken, basting with marinade as you do so. When almost ready, add pineapple and cook until well marked.

Serve each breast with 1 or 2 slices of pineapple.

'To easily cut fresh pineapple into rings, just use pastry cutters. First of all cut thick slices of pineapple, then use a large cutter to cut just inside the skin, followed by a small one to remove the core.'

Dear Huey...

>I would like to thank you for
your inspiration to my husband
who has recently discovered the
kitchen. He is a shiftworker
and, if not working, watches you
religiously of a weekday and
weekend. Thanks to you, he helps
in the kitchen and acknowledges
your style of cooking as he is
preparing food. Keep up the good
work and I'm sure my husband
will too.
Susan

>I'm a 19-year-old arts student
and a huge fan of your show. My housemates and I rarely
miss the show even though that means skipping a few
lectures. We'd love to see heaps more vegetarian recipes.
Sodapop VIC

>Just a short note to say that if you're going to leave
something to marinate for half an hour, you should make
sure there isn't a clock in the background. It was about
four and a half minutes by my count.
Great show.
Brett

>Do like your new look - was unsure at first - don't get
too fit and healthy - you'll be letting us eaters down!!!
Sharon

>I am 10 and in Grade 5. My class and I really love your
show. We like the way you cook the food and the way you
present the food. In our class we are learning about
healthy eating. It is very important to eat fruit
because fruit keeps your bones strong.
Ryan VIC

Glazed Roast Chicken with Orange, Honey & Hoisin

(SERVES 4–6)

2 heaped tbsp hoisin sauce
2 heaped tbsp honey, melted
1 heaped tbsp Dijon mustard
a splash of soy sauce
1 tspn sambal oelek
juice of 2 oranges

Preheat oven to highest degree.
Whisk together.

1 large chicken
3–4 sweet potatoes, peeled & cut into chunks
vegetable oil
freshly ground salt & pepper

Fold wings under chicken, push legs back and push skewer through thighs and tip of breast. Then toss sweet potatoes in a baking tray with a little oil and seasonings, move to sides and place chicken in middle. Then pour two thirds of the honey mix over.

Cook in oven for 10 minutes. Turn heat down to 200°C and cook for about another 50 minutes, regularly basting and adding the rest of the honey mix (and some water) as necessary.

'Not absolutely necessary, but some steamed green beans or broccoli would go well with this.'

Baby Chickens on Roasted Parsnips

(SERVES 4)

olive oil
4–6 parsnips, peeled & cut into chunks
freshly ground salt & pepper

Preheat oven to its highest degree. Pour a generous splash of olive oil into a baking tray, add parsnips and seasonings and toss well. Cook on stove top for 5 minutes tossing regularly.

4 baby chickens (poussins)
melted butter
1 lemon

Fold wings under chickens, push legs back and secure with a skewer through the thighs and tips of the breast. Put in tray (making sure parsnips are not underneath), generously brush with butter and season. Then squeeze lemon over each.

Cook on medium high rack in oven, for 20–25 minutes until juices run clear when you prick base of thigh with a fork, basting 2 or 3 times. Serve either whole or cut up with juices poured over the top.

'You could also use marylands of chicken for this. But do keep in mind that the maryland is actually a cut of chicken which incorporates both the thigh and drumstick and not that star of the sixties which involved deep-fried chicken with the odd piece of banana and pineapple.'

FURTHER THOUGHTS
on portioning a chicken

A whole chicken is often cheaper than the equivalent weight in chicken pieces — and it's not hard to cut into eight. But, be warned, you do need a sharp knife.

1   Place chicken, breast up, on a board. Pull leg away from body and cut through between body and leg. Push leg downwards until ball comes out of the joint and cut through. Repeat process with other leg. (This drumstick and thigh combination is called a maryland).

2   Put maryland flat on board and cut through the centre of the 'v', where the bones meet.

3   With breast still upwards, smooth out skin and cut down one side of the breast bone with knife. Keeping the knife against carcass, keep cutting until breast is free. Pull out wing and cut between breast and carcass to free. Cut off wing tip and set aside for stock. Repeat with other breast.

4   Cut breast crossways through the middle of breast.

5   Either use carcass, wing tips, etc. for stock if making it in the next day or two or put into the freezer, immediately, for later use.

A Quick Sauté of Chicken

(SERVES 4)

1 chicken, portioned (see opposite) plain flour olive oil	Lightly flour chicken and brown in hot oil. Remove.
8 chats, halved 8–12 button onions 2–3 medium carrots, peeled & cut in thick slices 1 tbsp paprika	Add to pan and cook for a few minutes.
2 tbsp plain flour	Add, mix well, turn down heat and cook for 2 minutes, regularly stirring.
1$\frac{1}{2}$ cups chicken stock, bought or homemade (see page 62) $\frac{1}{2}$ cup dry white wine freshly ground salt & pepper	Add, bring to the boil and stir well. Return chicken and cover pan. Then simmer very gently for about 30 minutes (adding more stock if necessary).
chopped fresh parsley	Serve sprinkled with parsley.

'For this a sauté pan would be best (yes, just like the one in the Huey's Kitchen range), but if not available any large pan with a lid would do.'

Chicken Pie with a Potato Crust
(SERVES 6)

6 large potatoes, peeled & cubed	Cook until tender and then drain.
1 tbsp vegetable oil	Preheat oven to 220°C.
1 tbsp butter	While the potatoes are cooking, heat oil and
1 large onion, sliced	butter in a heavy-bottomed pot and sauté
10 button mushrooms, sliced	vegies and bacon for about 5 minutes.
2 rindless bacon rashers, sliced	
10 chicken thighs, boned & cubed	Add and cook until chicken changes colour.
freshly ground salt & pepper	
3 tbsp flour	Add, turn down heat and cook for a few minutes.
2–3 cups of chicken stock, bought or homemade (see page 62)	Add and gently simmer until thick, stirring regularly.
2 tbsp cream	
1 tbsp chopped fresh parsley	
hot milk	While chicken is cooking, mash spuds with
freshly ground salt & pepper	a little hot milk. Then season.
	Put chicken mix in an ovenproof serving dish, top with mash and cook for about 20 minutes.

'Another of my mother's recipes. She often served it without the mash on a bed of rice.'

Peking Duck Wraps

(SERVES 4)

$^1/_2$ bought Chinese duck, boned

Wrap in foil and put on a grill or BBQ to reheat (or put in the oven). Then slice.

8 flour tortillas

Heat on grill or BBQ.

hoisin sauce
$^1/_4$ iceberg lettuce, sliced
2 spring (green) onions, halved lengthways
    & cut into 3–4 cm pieces
$^1/_4$ continental (telegraph) cucumber, cut in
    4 lengthways

Smear tortillas with hoisin, top with lettuce, spring onion, cucumber and duck, and roll up tightly. Cut each in half crossways to serve.

'The cheat's Peking duck.'

Chicken Stock

(MAKES 3–4 LITRES)

1 boiling fowl
2 kg chicken carcasses
2 onions, chopped
2 carrots, washed & chopped
2 leeks, washed & chopped
1 celery stalk, washed & chopped
5 litres cold water
3 fresh thyme sprigs
1 slice of lemon
1 bay leaf
4 whole black peppercorns

Section the fowl and chop the carcasses. Put in a stockpot along with everything else. Bring to the boil and simmer very, very gently for 3 hours, skimming frequently and topping up with more water if chicken becomes exposed. DO NOT STIR. Then strain, cool and refrigerate overnight.

Next day, remove fat from the surface.

'I remove the chicken flesh, shred it finely and mix it with mayonnaise for a great sandwich filling.'

Oven-Fried Lemon Chicken

(SERVES 4)

$^1/_2$ cup plain flour

2 tspn paprika

freshly ground salt

Preheat oven to 200°C.

Combine.

olive oil

a good knob of butter

1 large chicken, portioned (see page 58)

Heat oil and butter in a pan which can go into the oven. Flour chicken and cook until golden all over. Then bake in oven for 10 minutes.

$^1/_2$ cup fresh lemon juice

grated zest from 1 lemon

2 tbsp soy sauce

$^1/_2$ cup chicken stock, bought or homemade
   (see page 62)

freshly ground pepper

Put in a bowl, add any cooking juices and whisk. Pour over the chicken and cook for another 15 minutes turning once or twice. Serve with steamed greens or rice.

'Every one of my books has had at least one recipe from Des Britten. Des, who these days is Wellington's City Missioner, was chef-proprietor of New Zealand's famous Coachman Restaurant and was 'Swinging Dee' of radio fame. This is an old recipe of his, sent in by a viewer who obviously knew of my reputation as 'The Coachman's Kitchenhand from Hell.'

Roulade of Stuffed Chicken with Coriander & Lime Mayo

(SERVES 4)

vegetable oil
1 medium carrot, peeled & julienned
1 leek, well washed & julienned
2 celery stalks, julienned
soy sauce

Heat a little oil in a pot and gently sauté vegies for a few minutes. Add a little soy and cook for a few minutes more.

4 skinless chicken breasts

Flatten out chicken with a meat mallet. Then place a good spoonful of vegies crossways on breast and roll up. Wrap tightly in kitchen wrap twirling the ends like a bonbon and then wrap in foil. Cook in lightly boiling water for about 12–15 minutes until firm when squeezed. Then turn off heat and leave to cool in water.

6 tbsp mayonnaise, bought or homemade (see page 23)
3 tbsp sour cream
juice of 1–1$\frac{1}{2}$ limes
2 tbsp chopped fresh coriander

Mix together.

When cold, unwrap and slice chicken. Serve with the mayo on the side (and a green salad).

'I cooked this for our Melbourne Cup special on **Huey's TV Dinner** and was pleasantly surprised at the Mornington Races where a number of people came up to me and showed their versions which they had brought to the races for lunch.'

Lemony Turkey Rissoles

(SERVES 4)

500 g minced turkey meat

1 cup breadcrumbs

freshly ground salt & pepper

1 tspn paprika

$^1/_2$ tspn ground cumin

2 tbsp chopped fresh parsley

3 tbsp fresh lemon juice

2–3 spring (green) onions, chopped

Mix well. If too dry, add 1 egg and if too moist, add a little flour.

plain flour

olive oil

Form into patties, flour and cook in moderately hot oil until golden brown on both sides. Remove and set aside.

1 medium onion, chopped

1 garlic clove, crushed

Add a little more oil if necessary and sauté vegies.

$1^1/_2$ cups chicken stock, bought or
   homemade (see page 62)

1–2 tbsp fresh lemon juice

a good splash of cream

1 tbsp chopped fresh parsley

freshly ground salt

Tabasco, to taste

Add and simmer until thickish. Return rissoles and cook very gently until cooked through, turning once or twice (and adding more stock if necessary).

sliced spring (green) onion

couscous (see page 248) or steamed rice

Mound couscous or rice on plates, top with rissoles, sauce and spring onion.

'Of course you could use chicken mince.'

The Original Warm Chicken Salad

(SERVES 4–6)

³/₄ cup vegetable oil
1 heaped tspn sambal oelek
1 garlic clove, crushed
freshly ground salt & pepper
a splash of soy sauce

Whisk together in a bowl. Set aside one third.

2–3 skinless chicken breasts

Toss in marinade and leave for 30 minutes, turning once or twice.

8 cooked baby potatoes, halved
2 corn cobs, cooked & cut into thick slices
4 rindless bacon rashers

Preheat BBQ.
Put chicken breasts on barbie along with potatoes and corn. Cook, turning regularly, adding bacon towards the end.

1 large handful mixed lettuces
1 punnet cherry tomatoes, halved

Slice chicken and bacon and toss along with lettuces, tomatoes, potatoes and corn. Add reserved marinade to taste and serve in a large bowl with plenty of crusty bread on the side.

'As I mentioned before, this was the first recipe I presented on **Healthy, Wealthy & Wise**, where it was a huge success.'

Vietnamese Ginger & Lemongrass Chicken

(SERVES 4)

1–2 lemongrass stalks, finely sliced 1 tbsp freshly grated ginger $^1/_4$ cup vegetable oil	Whiz up in a blender or processor.
3–4 skinless chicken breasts, cubed	Add to above and marinate for 30 minutes.
$^1/_2$ red onion, finely sliced 2 garlic cloves, crushed 2 chillies, finely sliced	Pour some of the oil from chicken into wok and heat. Stirfry onion, garlic and chillies for 10 seconds.
$1^1/_2$ tbsp Asian fish sauce $^1/_2$ cup chicken stock, bought or homemade (see page 62) a good pinch of sugar sea salt, to taste	Add along with drained chicken and cook very gently for 7–8 minutes.
3 tbsp chopped fresh coriander 2 spring (green) onions, cut into 3 cm lengths	Add and toss well to just wilt spring onion.
steamed rice	Serve on rice with juices poured over.

 'Unfortunately, my favourite piece of kitchen equipment, the Microplane grater, is already patented so it cannot become a part of the Huey's Kitchen range. But it is the perfect grater for ginger, garlic, lemongrass and the like and, interestingly enough, began life as a woodworking tool.'

Spicy Mandarin Chicken Drumsticks

(SERVES 4)

2 tbsp vegetable oil 2 tspn freshly grated ginger 4 whole dried chillies 2 fresh chillies, seeded & finely sliced 2 tspn green peppercorns, drained	Heat a little oil in a wok and briefly toss.
8–12 chicken drumsticks	Add and cook for 2–3 minutes until the chicken changes colour.
$^1/_3$ cup fresh mandarin juice 1/2 cup chicken stock, bought or homemade (see page 62) 3–4 tbsp soy sauce 2 mandarins, segmented	Add and gently cook for about 15 minutes until chicken is cooked, turning regularly and adding more stock if necessary. Remove chicken to a bowl.
a pinch of sugar 4 spring (green) onions, cut into 3 cm lengths	Add and cook for 1 minute. Then pour over chicken.
steamed rice	Serve with rice.

'This is a variation on a recipe by Charmaine Solomon who, to my mind, is the guru of all things Asian.'

FURTHER THOUGHTS
on bought BBQ chickens

★ Make a paste with oil, sambal oelek, honey and soy. Halve or quarter the chicken, generously brush with paste and put under an overhead grill until piping hot and bubbling.

★ Cut boned chook into pieces and toss with sautéed bacon, hot boiled potato, a variety of leaves and whatever green vegies take your fancy. Dress with your favourite vinaigrette.

★ Shred and toss with bean shoots, sliced baby carrots, snowpeas, red onion, cubed avocado, shredded iceberg and lots of spicy Nam Jim sauce (see page 96).

★ Remove from bone, cut into chunks and toss in a Caesar salad, along with grilled bacon, cos leaves, shaved parmesan and anchovy mayo (see page 51).

★ Cut into 4, wrap in foil with a generous sprinkling of lemon juice and heat on the BBQ or in the oven. Serve on a bed of blanched green beans with a sprinkling of cucumber raita (see page 9).

★ Make a pesto mayonnaise by combining mayonnaise with pesto — either a good bought or homemade (see page 42). Then shred chicken, mix through and stuff into a baguette.

★ Place cooked spaghetti in a deep baking dish. Top with shredded chicken and mornay sauce (see page 86) to which you have added a splash of sherry. Sprinkle with grated tasty cheese and bake until golden and bubbling.

Grilled Sardines with Turkish Carrot Mash • Blue Eye 'Kiev' • John Dory with Spring Onion & Lemon Sauce • Smoked Cod Pie • Philip Johnson's Cuttlefish & Chorizo Sausage with Chickpeas, Tomatoes & Chilli • Fish & Chip Butty • Crispy Fried Fish with Sweet Chilli Sauce Omelette Arnold Bennett • A Good Old-Fashioned Tuna Mornay • Seared Tuna with Greek Fetta Cheese Salad • Kedgeree • Vincent Poon's Seafood Laksa • Szechuan Snapper • Cantonese-Style Steamed Fish BBQ Hapuka with Leeks, Lemon & Dill • Fish Stock • Fish Meuniere • Thai Salmon Cakes with Thai Vinaigrette • A Parcel of Salmon & Fennel Moroccan Seafood Stew

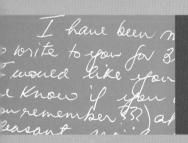

Dishes of Fishes

I must admit our family were never great fishermen (or is that now fisherpersons?). In fact, I can never remember us catching anything. Although I do remember my brother Don (circa 1960) once catching my finger with his hook during a highly complicated casting process.

But, our family did have one saving grace – they could cook the blessed stuff. Whether it was my mother simply lightly flouring fillets before slipping them into a small amount of hot oil and butter; or my father whipping up his famous beer batter; or us kids wrapping cutlets in foil and bunging them in the oven, the seafood in the Hewitson household was invariably delicious.

And, let's be honest, there was only really one secret – the freshness of the fish was of paramount importance.

So, don't be scared of cooking seafood at home. Simply become a regular at the reputable fishmongers and, do as my mother did, ask and follow his or her advice as to what is at its best today (and may I also add this quote from New York's Oscar Gizelt, of Delmonico's Restaurant fame, which, to me, says it all: 'Fish should smell like the tide. Once they smell like fish, it's too late').

Grilled Sardines with Turkish Carrot Mash

(SERVES 4)

4–6 large carrots, peeled & sliced	Preheat ridged grill or BBQ. Boil until tender. Then drain and coarsely mash.
$^1/_4$ tspn each of ground cumin, paprika, chilli powder & turmeric 1 garlic clove, crushed a good squeeze of fresh lemon juice $^1/_2$ tbsp honey 2 tbsp chopped fresh parsley freshly ground salt 2 tbsp olive oil	Mix in well to carrot mash and keep hot.
16–20 large sardines olive oil freshly ground salt 1 lemon	Brush sardines with oil, season with salt and lemon and grill in 2 or 3 lots, brushing with oil and squeezing more lemon juice over the top as you do so.
chopped fresh parsley	Put a mound of carrot mash on plates and top with 4 or 5 sardines. Sprinkle with parsley.

'I am now told that what we commonly refer to as sardines in Australia are in fact pilchards. But whatever their name, they are under-rated, reasonably priced and should be part of every Aussie barbie. (Just keep in mind that the grill needs to be oiled really well beforehand, as they do tend to stick a little.)'

Blue Eye 'Kiev'

(SERVES 4)

100 g unsalted butter, softened
2 garlic cloves, crushed
a squeeze of fresh lemon juice
1 heaped tbsp chopped fresh parsley

Mix together and put in a piping bag.

8 x 100 g thickish blue eye steaks with skin,
  bones removed

With a thin sharp knife, separate part of the skin from the fish and pipe a little butter in. Then smooth skin down and put in refrigerator for 1 hour.

plain flour
breadcrumbs
1/2 cup milk
1 egg

Preheat oven to 200°C.
Put flour, crumbs and milk whisked with egg in 3 separate bowls. Then carefully dust fish with flour, dip into egg wash and press firmly in crumbs.

olive oil

Heat a thin layer of oil in a large pan which can go into the oven and gently cook fish on both sides until lightly golden. Then put in oven to finish cooking.

tartare sauce (see below)
fresh lemon wedges

Drain well and serve with tartare and lemon.

'To make tartare sauce, to 1 cup of mayonnaise (homemade will make it even better, see page 23), add a generous squeeze of lemon, 1 tablespoon chopped capers, 2 chopped gherkins, 2 tablespoons chopped fresh parsley and 1 tablespoon very finely chopped red onion.'

John Dory with Spring Onion & Lemon Sauce

(SERVES 1 OR 2)

1 John Dory, head & fins removed
plain flour
1 tspn ground cumin
table salt

Mix together a little flour, cumin and salt. Then coat fish and shake off any excess.

olive oil
a knob of butter
freshly ground salt & pepper

Heat a little oil and butter in a large pan and carefully add fish. Season and gently cook over a moderate heat, turning once and basting regularly. When cooked, remove to a serving plate.

1 lemon, peeled, seeded & diced
2 spring (green) onions, sliced
1 tbsp chopped fresh parsley
a good dollop of butter

Add to pan, swirl around a few times and pour over the fish.

Beetroot Chips, optional (see page 242)

'One of the most important things to remember when cooking fish is that it will continue to cook once it has been removed from the heat source. So keep it a little undercooked and to check, simply make a small cut with a thin, sharp knife.'

Smoked Cod Pie

(SERVES 6–8)

3–4 smoked cod fillets
milk
2 parsley sprigs
2 bay leaves

Preheat oven to 200°C.
Cut each fillet in 3 crossways and put in a large pan. Generously cover with milk, add parsley and bay leaves and bring to the boil. Cover, turn off heat and leave for 10 minutes, turning after 5 minutes. Remove fish and strain liquid.

2–3 tbsp butter
2–3 tbsp plain flour

In a large pot, melt butter, add flour and mix in well. Cook over a low heat for a few minutes and add the strained poaching liquid and whisk vigorously. Then gently cook until thick, whisking regularly. Turn off heat.

grated tasty cheese
cream
freshly ground salt & pepper

Add a handful of cheese, a good splash of cream and seasoning to taste.

4 handfuls of baby spinach, well washed
4–6 ripe tomatoes, cored & sliced
6 hard boiled eggs, sliced

2 spring (green) onions, chopped
2 tbsp chopped fresh parsley
grated tasty cheese

Put spinach in a colander and pour boiling water over the top. Toss, drain well and put in bottom of a large gratin dish. Top with tomato, eggs and a sprinkling of cheese sauce.

Remove bones and skin from fish and flake. Fold into remaining cheese sauce, along with parsley and spring onion, and pour over the top of eggs. Generously sprinkle with cheese and bake for about 20 minutes, until golden and bubbling.

'I couldn't believe it when the boys at Bi-Lo told me how much smoked cod they sell. But after featuring some dishes on **Huey's Cooking Adventures**, all of which were very popular, it appears there are tons of smoked cod lovers out there (or soon will be).'

FURTHER THOUGHTS
on buying fish

★ The eyes should be clear, bright and bulging, the gills should be brightly coloured, the skin should be shiny and scaly and the flesh should feel firm and resilient to the touch.

★ The best fillets or cutlets will always be those that are cut from the fish right there in front of you (and, if at all possible, ensure that this is the case). But when pre-cut, they should also be firm and resilient with a fresh, translucent colour. And, above all, they should not be sitting in a pool of liquid.

★ A fresh clean smell is essential. Fresh fish should smell of the sea. It should not smell 'fishy', have even a whiff of ammonia (except in the case of skate) or appear musty or pungent.

★ So, beware of fish which either has opaque, concave eyes, is faded in colour, has soft flesh or has even the slightest unpleasant odour.

★ And, last but not least, if you have to travel any distance with your purchase, either keep it on ice or in an esky, as it spoils very very easily.

Philip Johnson's Cuttlefish & Chorizo Sausage with Chickpeas, Tomatoes & Chilli

(SERVES 2)

4–6 pieces cuttlefish or squid tube

With a sharp, thin knife, score in a diamond pattern.

olive oil
freshly ground salt & pepper
1 chorizo sausage, sliced

Heat oil in a large pan, add seasonings, then cuttlefish (cut side down) and cook quickly. Turn over, add chorizo and lightly cook on both sides.

2 handfuls of mizuna lettuce
1 large chilli, seeded & sliced
8 cherry tomatoes, halved
2 tspn Italian (flat leaf) parsley,
   roughly chopped
zest & juice of 1 lemon
4 heaped tbsp canned chickpeas,
   drained & rinsed

At the same time, toss salad and mound on plates. Then top with cuttlefish and chorizo and pour any pan juices over the top.

'Cuttlefish is regarded both by the Japanese and Chinese as superior to the more common squid. But, whether or not this is simply because it is in shorter supply, I'm not sure. (I also am intrigued by one of its Chinese names 'foo ban woo chak', which I'm told means 'tiger blotched black thief'.)'

Fish & Chip Butty

(SERVES 4)

2–3 large floury potatoes, peeled	Cut into thick chips lengthways. Then place under running water and leave until the water runs clear. Drain and dry carefully.
6 cups vegetable oil	Heat oil in a wok to 160°C (see page 15) and cook chips for 4–5 minutes until lightly coloured, but not brown. Drain well and set aside.
$^{1}/_{2}$ stubby of lager, freshly opened cold water a good pinch salt 1 tspn baking powder 175–200 g self-raising flour	Put beer in a large bowl along with half as much water. Mix salt, baking powder and flour together and add to the liquid, little by little, continually whisking. When batter coats your finger lightly, it is ready. Set aside.
table salt	Reheat oil to 180°–190°C and fry chips until golden. Drain well, sprinkle with salt and keep hot in oven.
8 x 80 g pieces of boneless skinless fish	Then dip fish pieces into batter and fry in 2 lots until golden. Drain well.
fresh tomato sauce (see page 219) tartare sauce, bought or homemade (see page 75) 1 baguette	Cut baguette into 4 crossways and then in half lengthways. Smear base with tartare, top with fish, chips and tomato sauce and press lid on.

'This is my father's famous crispy beer batter which is a popular request every time it has featured on my shows. And the butty – well this was a favourite in our family, particularly when some of my mother's homemade tomato sauce was available (but when it wasn't we did tend to make do with the commercial variety).'

Crispy Fried Fish with Sweet Chilli Sauce

(SERVES 4)

1 cup white vinegar
$^1/_2$ cup caster sugar
$^1/_2$ tspn salt

Put in a pot and simmer for a couple of minutes, to dissolve sugar.

3 chillies, finely chopped
3 garlic cloves, finely chopped
1 tspn freshly grated ginger
$^1/_4$ cup crushed pineapple

Add, mix well and set aside.

6 cups vegetable oil
8 x 80 gm fresh boneless fish fillets
beer batter (see page 82)
fresh lime wedges

Heat oil in a wok or deep sided pot to 190°C (see page 15).
Dip fish in batter, drain off a little and put in oil, holding on until it floats. Cook, turning until golden, then drain well on paper towels. Salt lightly and serve with sauce and lime on the side.

'A terrific, simple sweet chilli sauce.'

Omelette Arnold Bennett

(SERVES 2–4)

poached smoked cod & strained cooking liquid (see page 78)	Skin, bone and flake.
1 tbsp butter 1 tbsp plain flour freshly ground salt & pepper	Melt butter in a pot, add flour and gently cook for 1–2 minutes. Then add 1 cup cooking liquid and seasonings. Whisk well and cook gently until thick.
1 tspn Dijon mustard $1/4$ cup grated tasty cheese 1 heaped tbsp chopped fresh parsley	Add, mix well and turn off heat. Preheat overhead grill.
8 large eggs	Whisk in a bowl and add flaked cod and most of the cheese sauce.
a good knob of butter	Heat in a large non-stick pan, add cod mix and let bubble for a few minutes, shaking the pan. Turn heat down, cover and cook very gently until cooked, but still runny in the centre.
grated tasty cheese	Top with rest of cheese sauce and more grated cheese and slip under overhead grill until lightly browned. Serve for lunch with a green salad.

'Created for British novelist Arnold Bennett (1867–1931) at the famed Mirabelle Restaurant in London (now owned by British wunderkind, Marco Pierre White), where it is said that he ate it every day for ten years.'

A Good Old-Fashioned Tuna Mornay

(SERVES 4)

¼ cup freshly grated parmesan
¼ cup breadcrumbs
2 tbsp chopped fresh parsley
freshly ground salt & pepper

Preheat oven to 200°C.
Combine and set aside.

3 tbsp butter
3 tbsp plain flour
2 cups milk, hot

Put butter in a pot and melt. Add flour, mix
in well and cook over a low heat for a few
minutes. Then add milk, whisking vigorously.
Cook until thick and turn off heat.

grated tasty cheese
a splash of cream
4 spring (green) onions, chopped
freshly ground salt & pepper

Add a good handful of cheese, plus the
cream, onions and seasonings to taste.

850 g canned tuna, drained & separated into
  largish chunks

Fold in gently and pour into a gratin dish.
Sprinkle crumb mix over the top and cook in
the oven for 15–20 minutes, keeping an eye
on the crumbs. (If browning too much,
cover with foil.)

Serve with a green salad.

 'Forget the crumb mix if you like and just put extra cheese
on the top. You can also add vegies such as corn, green peas,
diced carrots, etc. to make it into a real one-pot wonder.'

Seared Tuna with Greek Fetta Cheese Salad

(SERVES 4)

$^1/_2$ cup extra virgin olive oil
juice of $^1/_2$ lemon
1 garlic clove, crushed
1–2 tspn chopped fresh oregano
freshly ground salt & pepper

Whisk together and set half aside for
a dressing.

4 x 180 g tuna steaks, bloodline removed

Marinate for 20 minutes in half of above.

$^1/_2$ red onion, finely sliced
3 ripe tomatoes, cored & cut into wedges
$^1/_2$ red capsicum, cored, seeded & finely sliced
10 pitted black olives, halved
150 g fetta cheese, crumbled

While tuna is marinating, toss salad
ingredients with reserved dressing to
taste and mound on 4 plates.

On a preheated grill or BBQ, sear tuna over
a high heat to, at the most, medium-rare,
brushing with marinade as you do so.
Place on salad and sprinkle with any left
over dressing.

'Always regard tuna as the steak of the sea and cook it,
at the most, medium-rare. Otherwise it will be dry and
tasteless. Also lash out a bit and buy the best sashimi
grade – the difference is remarkable.'

Kedgeree

(SERVES 4–6)

500 g smoked cod

milk

1/4 onion, sliced

1 bay leaf

1 parsley sprig

a few whole black peppercorns

Put cod in a pan, generously cover with milk, add aromatics and bring to the boil. Cover, turn off the heat and leave for 10 minutes, turning after 5 minutes. Remove fish and strain liquid.

olive oil

1 large onion, chopped

2 garlic cloves, crushed

1 celery stalk, diced

1 medium carrot, diced

In a pot heat a little oil and sauté vegies until browned around the edges.

2 heaped tspn curry powder

1 tspn turmeric

Add, stir and cook for 1–2 minutes.

200 g basmati rice

Add, along with 600 ml of the cod poaching liquid, and mix well. Tightly cover and cook very gently until rice is tender (about 10–12 minutes), adding more liquid if necessary.

2 tbsp chopped fresh coriander

4 hard boiled eggs, peeled & quartered

Indian mango chutney

fresh coriander sprigs

Remove skin and bones from fish, flake and fold through rice with coriander. Put in a large bowl and garnish with eggs, chutney and coriander.

'Kedgeree, an Anglo–Indian dish, is derived from the Indian breakfast dish 'khichri', which was traditionally made with mung beans and rice. The flaked fish and hard boiled eggs were added during the days of the Raj to appeal to English tastes and, to this day, it is still a popular British breakfast dish. Although I prefer it for lunch with a tangy green salad.'

Vincent Poon's Seafood Laksa

(SERVES 6–8)

3 red capsicum, cored, seeded & chopped
1 tbsp curry powder
1 tspn paprika
1/2 cup vegetable oil

Whiz up in a blender or processor. Then put in a pot and fry until almost dry. Remove from heat.

1 red onion, chopped
5 red chillies, seeded & chopped
1 tbsp sambal oelek
1 tbsp table salt
1 tbsp brown sugar

Whiz up in processor and add to pot.

2 lemongrass stalks, cleaned & cut into 3 crossways
2 litres fish stock, bought or homemade (see page 94)
3 cups coconut cream

Add, turn heat back on and bring to a simmer. Gently cook for 15 minutes.

12 green prawns, peeled & deveined
400 g mixture of boneless fish fillets, cubed
12–16 mussels in the shell
8 large scallops

Add everything except scallops and gently simmer until cooked (removing to bowl as they are ready). Turn heat off, throw in scallops and leave while you prepare bowls.

Hokkien noodles, soaked in hot water for 10 minutes then drained
bean shoots
sliced spring (green) onions
coriander, chopped fresh
sliced iceberg lettuce

Put in large bowls along with seafood and pour laksa over the top.

coriander sprigs
lime wedges

Garnish with coriander and serve with lime on the side.

'This is supposedly a soup but, to my mind, it's a meal in itself and should be treated as such.'

Szechuan Snapper

(SERVES 2)

2 x 200 g snapper, steaks or cutlets
Chinese wine
light soy sauce

Half fill a large wok with water, top with a large bamboo steamer and bring water to the boil. Place fish on a plate which will fit into steamer and generously sprinkle with wine and soy. Put in steamer, cover and cook. (To check when ready, make a cut with a small sharp knife.)

3 tbsp peanut oil
3 tspn sesame oil
1 garlic clove, crushed
$^1/_2$ tspn freshly grated ginger
1 heaped tspn Asian chilli bean sauce
2 spring (green) onions, finely chopped

When fish is ready, heat oils until smoking in a small pan. Then carefully mix in other ingredients along with fish cooking juices.

2 bok choy heads steamed
steamed rice

Place bok choy on plates, top with fish and pour oil mix over the top. Serve with rice on the side.

'Szechuan is one of the four major cooking styles of China. This is the cuisine of the aromatics with the food invariably being robust and often (but not always) hot and spicy.'

Cantonese-Style Steamed Fish

(SERVES 1 OR 2)

1 whole plate–sized fish, scaled & cleaned
1 tspn freshly grated ginger
Japanese soy sauce

Fill a wok to one third full with water and put a large bamboo steamer on top. When boiling, put fish on a plate (which will fit into steamer) and sprinkle with ginger and a generous amount of soy. Place in steamer, put lid on, and cook until almost ready (to check, make a small cut behind the head).

2–3 spring (green) onions, sliced

Throw on the top, cover and cook for a few seconds.

steamed rice

Place fish on a platter and pour all juices over the top. Serve with steamed rice.

 'Excuse me for repeating this recipe (it was featured in **Tales and Recipes from a Travelling Cook**), but this is one of the true classics of fish cooking – both simple and failsafe. And it also works just as well with fish steaks or cutlets.'

BBQ Hapuka with Leeks, Lemon & Dill

(SERVES 4)

8 small leeks, well washed & cut in half
   crossways

Preheat BBQ or grill.
Blanch in plenty of boiling water until
crisp-tender then drain well.

4 x 180 g hapuka steaks
olive oil
freshly ground salt & pepper
1 lemon

Lightly brush fish with oil, season and cook
along with leeks on oiled BBQ, squeezing
lemon juice over the top as you do so.

dill, chopped fresh
extra virgin olive oil
lemon wedges

To serve, place leeks on a plate, top with fish
and sprinkle with dill and olive oil.

'Any 'steaky' fish such as blue eye, snapper, yellowtail or, my favourite
barramundi, will do.'

Fish Stock

(MAKES 2 LITRES)

2 kg fish bones, including heads
2 onions, roughly chopped
1 celery stalk, chopped
1 medium carrot, chopped
2 leeks, well washed & chopped
2 tbsp olive oil
2 garlic cloves, chopped
10 black peppercorns
2 bay leaves
4 parsley stalks
2.5 litres of water
500 ml dry white wine

Thoroughly wash bones, removing all traces of blood. Then take out eyes and gills and wash heads well. Chop bones into 10 cm lengths.

Heat oil in a large heavy-bottomed pot, add vegies and gently sauté for 5 minutes. Add bones, peppercorns, bay leaves and parsley and toss for a few more minutes. Add liquid and bring to the boil. Skim off foam and simmer for 20 minutes, skimming frequently.

Turn off and stand for another 20 minutes, before straining.

Fish Meuniere

(SERVES 4)

8 x 100 g boneless, skinless fish fillets
freshly ground salt & pepper
plain flour

Season fish and lightly dust with flour.

olive oil
a good knob of butter

Put in a large pan and heat. Shake off any excess flour from fish, slip into oil and carefully cook over a moderate heat until golden on both sides. (To check if it's ready, make a small cut.) Remove to serving plates.

another good knob of butter
juice of 1–2 lemons
1–2 tbsp chopped fresh parsley

Add butter, lemon juice and parsley to hot pan. Swirl to combine and pour over fish.

Serve with some steamed greens and boiled potatoes.

'Another of the real basics and pretty failsafe too, as long as you don't allow the pan to get too hot. And keep in mind that when a recipe is as simple as this the freshness and sheer quality of the prime ingredient is of the utmost importance (see page 80).'

Thai Salmon Cakes with Thai Vinaigrette

(SERVES 8)

2 garlic cloves, chopped

2 coriander roots, well washed & finely
   chopped

1 tspn rock salt

1 tspn caster sugar

4 chillies, seeded & chopped

2 tbsp Asian fish sauce

Preheat oven to 220°C.
Make a Thai 'vinaigrette' by whizzing these
ingredients up in the processor.

4–6 tbsp lime juice

3 tbsp chopped fresh coriander

Then mix this in, keeping in mind that the
sauce should hit you in the face. Set aside.

$^1/_2$ large red capsicum, cored, seeded
   & coarsely chopped

1 cm piece of ginger, finely sliced

2 garlic cloves, finely sliced

3 tbsp Asian chilli sauce

Whiz up in processor.

500 g fresh salmon offcuts or scraps 100 ml coconut cream	Add and process until smooth.
1 egg a pinch of salt	Add and whiz for a few more seconds.
6 spring (green) onions, chopped 1/2 bunch coriander leaves, well washed & chopped	Put fish mix in a bowl, mix in greens and form into patties about 7 cm in diameter.
vegetable oil plain flour	Heat a little oil in a pan which can go into the oven. Flour and cook patties on both sides. Then cook in oven until firm to the touch turning over once.
continental (telegraph) cucumber, skin on & sliced	To serve, place cucumber on plates, top with patties and sprinkle over sauce.

'You can also make these with other varieties of fish.'

A Parcel of Salmon & Fennel

(SERVES 4)

2–3 small fennel bulbs, finely sliced
chicken stock, bought or homemade
   (see page 62)
olive oil
freshly ground salt & pepper

foil
4 x 180 g salmon steaks, skin
   & bones removed
fresh chervil

extra virgin olive oil
extra fresh chervil

Preheat BBQ or grill.
Put fennel in a pot, add stock to just cover
and add a generous splash of oil and
seasonings. Gently poach until just tender
and strain.

Cut 4 large squares of foil. Place on a bench,
shiny side out, and generously brush inside
with poaching liquid. Top with fish, a
mound of fennel, a few chervil sprigs and
a sprinkling of poaching liquid. Season
and tightly wrap up.

Cook parcels on moderate part of grill
or BBQ for 5 minutes or so. (To check if
cooked, make a small cut.) Then place on
plates, pour juices over the top and sprinkle
with a little oil. Garnish with chervil.

'Australians, except those with a Mediterranean
background, sadly tend to have little regard for fennel.
Which is a shame, because it is a delicious vegie. But
just in case you have been put off because it appears 'woody', you can
cut out and discard the core and always slice it very finely.'

Hi Hewy – Baby!

I really like your show. We enjoy your cooking show because it is always interesting. Our class is learning about healthy food. And I know that healthy food is good for all of us. Your show always makes me hungry. Thank you for the show.
Jessica VIC

I have been meaning to write to you for 3 years. I would like to know if you ate at a very pleasant seafood restaurant in Eugene Oregon USA mid-1997 or 1998. I can't remember the name but I kept staring at the fellow at the next table who I thought was you but did not like approaching him in case it wasn't. If it wasn't you then you have an absolute double. Am enclosing a stamped addressed envelope as you are busy I know – just tear off a scrap of paper and say yay or nay.
Norma QLD

I am writing to you on behalf of my mother who has recently retired and is finding it very difficult with all the extra time to get through the day. After caring for my father, her six children, her grandson, maintaining the house and working for more than 40 years, she finds it difficult to relax, even though she deserves to after all that time. She religiously watches you every weekday and says, 'I can get through the day now that I've watched Huey,' and she often quotes you when not only cooking, but talking to us and offering advice. She freely admits to having a crush on you! Can we have an autographed photo of yourself for her sixtieth birthday?
The Byrne family NSW

Moroccan Seafood Stew

(SERVES 2)

olive oil
½ red capsicum, cored, seeded & diced
½ red onion, diced
1 garlic clove, crushed

Heat a little oil in a wok and gently sauté vegies for a few minutes.

1 tspn turmeric
1 tspn paprika
1 heaped tspn sambal oelek

Add and toss well.

800 g canned diced tomatoes, drained a little
½ cup dry white wine
1 tspn honey
freshly ground salt & pepper
2 tbsp chopped fresh coriander

Add and cook until thickish and fragrant.

1 x 160 g salmon steak halved, skin & bones removed
2 x 70 g pieces of blue eye

Turn down heat and add fish. Cook for 3–4 minutes, covered.

6–8 mussels, scrubbed & debearded
4–6 large scallops
1 squid tube, cleaned & cut into rings (see page 7)

To debeard a mussel grasp the string-like substance that grows out of the side of the shell and pull it towards the hinge end until it comes away. Then add mussels, cover and cook, removing to deep bowls as the shells open (along with fish when cooked). Towards the end, add scallops and squid and briefly cook. Then check sauce seasoning and pour into bowls.

'Use any variety of seafood that you like and serve with plenty of crusty bread to mop up the juices.'

Bedi's Rogan Josh • Madhur Jaffrey's Perfect Rice Pilaf • Tagine of Lamb Chops with Tea-Soaked Prunes • Navarin of Lamb Riblets • Lamb Shank Hotch Potch • Moussaka • Mini Lamb Roast with Potatoes, Garlic & Rosemary • South African Sosaties Roast Leg of Lamb, Greek Style • Braised Lamb Shanks • Braised, Stuffed Forequarter of Lamb • Lancashire Hot Pot • Barbecued Rump of Beef with Charred Onion Salad • Mustard-Crusted Fillet of Beef with Minted Green Pea Puree • Steak Sandwich with Pesto • A Classic Pepper Steak with Sautéed Potatoes • Two Minute Steak with Date Salad T-Bones with Chimichurri Sauce • Fillet Steak with Blackbeans & Snowpeas • Beef Stock • Greek Beef Stew • Lamb's Fry with Onions & Sage • Steak & Kidney Pie • Pot au Feu of Tongue • Corned Beef with Mustard Sauce • Spice-Rubbed Rib Eye of Beef Shin of Veal in Red Wine with Crushed Potatoes • Baby Veal Cutlets with Microwave Blue Cheese Polenta • Parmentier's Hash • Beef Chili with Beer • Moroccan Keftas in Tomato & Preserved Lemon Sauce • American Meatball Sandwich All American Meatloaf • Pork Chops with Apples & Dry Apple Cider Glaze • Rack of Pork with Roasted Pears • Japanese Braised Pork Fillet • BBQ Baby Back Ribs with Coca-Cola Sauce • Pork Chops with Macaroni & Corn Cheese • Roast Pork with Crispy Crackling & Apple Gravy • Bacon, Egg & Tomato Pie • Sausages with Brussels Sprout Colcannon Cakes • Cabbage, Cheese & Sausage Bake Black Pudding with Champ & Beetroot Chutney

Make Mine Meat

My early memories of dining out always involve plates piled high with meat of one sort or over. Invariably badly trimmed and over-cooked, the accompaniments were little more than the odd French fry (or jacket potato), a wedge of tomato and, if you were lucky, a small pile of decidedly ordinary coleslaw.

Thankfully those days are long gone. But while few of us would consider ourselves to be quite the carnivores of yesteryear, it is interesting to note that the requests for meat recipes have continued to be high, with many viewers admonishing me for the fact that I don't present enough real Aussie tucker – steaks, chops and the like. Although, I must add that vegetarians also admonish me for not presenting enough vegetarian food, dessert lovers do the same about the lack of sweet courses and, the most aggressive of the lot – chocoholics – wouldn't be satisfied unless every course involved chocolate in one form or other.

Bedi's Rogan Josh

(SERVES 6)

vegetable oil	Heat a little oil in a large heavy-bottomed
2 large onions, chopped	pot and, over moderate heat, brown onion.
3 bay leaves	Add and stir well for 1–2 minutes.
1 cinnamon stick	
4 whole cardamon pods	
8 cloves	
10 black peppercorns	
2 tbsp finely chopped ginger	Add, stir and cook for 5 minutes.
1 tbsp finely chopped garlic	
1 tspn turmeric	
2 tbsp ground coriander	
1 tbsp cumin seeds	
1 tspn mace	
1 tspn chilli powder	
5 tomatoes, pureed	Add tomato, stir through and then add
1 cup yoghurt	yoghurt and lamb. Mix well and cook on
1 kg cubed, lean lamb	high heat for 20 minutes, occasionally
	stirring.
1$\frac{1}{4}$ cups water	Add, turn down heat and simmer for
	30 minutes.
chopped fresh coriander	Add coriander and serve with rice pilaf.
Rice Pilaf, optional (see page 105)	

'When Davinder Bedi cooked this on the show, I was surprised at the number and variety of spices used in what is essentially a rather mild dish. But it did explain the richness and depth of flavour of a good Rogan Josh.'

Madhur Jaffrey's Perfect Rice Pilaf

(SERVES 6–8)

Basmati rice to the 450 ml level in a
    measuring jug

Pick over rice and put in a bowl. Wash
under running water until water runs clear
and then drain. Cover with 1.25 litres of
water and leave for 30 minutes. Drain in a
sieve or colander and leave for 20 minutes.

3 tbsp vegetable oil
50 g finely chopped onion
$^1/_2$ chilli, finely sliced
$^1/_2$ tspn finely chopped garlic
$^1/_2$ tspn garam masala
1 tspn salt

Heat oil in a heavy-bottomed pot and
gently sauté onion until soft. Add rice and
rest of ingredients and gently cook,
regularly stirring, for 3–4 minutes.

600 ml chicken stock, bought or homemade
    (see page 62)

Add to pot and bring to the boil. Then
cover with foil and a tight fitting lid, turn
heat down to very, very low and cook for
15 minutes (and don't peek).

'Picking over rice simply means to check that there are no little foreign numbers,
such as tiny pebbles, etc. lurking (this does, on rare occasions, occur).'

Tagine of Lamb Chops with Tea-Soaked Prunes

(SERVES 4)

8–12 prunes prepared tea fresh orange juice	Soak prunes overnight in equal quantities of tea and orange juice.
olive oil 12 midloin lamb chops, trimmed well plain flour	Heat oil in a large heavy-bottomed pot, flour chops and seal. Remove.
1 large onion, chopped 2 garlic cloves, crushed	Add, along with more oil if necessary, and sauté until soft.
1 tbsp chopped fresh parsley 1 tbsp chopped fresh coriander 1 tbsp chopped fresh mint $1/2$ tspn turmeric $1/2$ tspn cumin $1/2$ tspn cinnamon 2 tspn sambal oelek 2 tbsp honey $3/4$ cup chicken stock, bought or homemade (see page 62) $1/2$ cup dry white wine freshly ground salt	Add, mix in well and bring to the boil. Then add lamb, cover and gently simmer for 40–50 minutes, turning meat every now and then.
lemon juice couscous (see page 248)	When chops are tender, add prunes and lemon juice to taste. Simmer for a few minutes, then serve with couscous.

'A tagine is a conical-topped cooking vessel (the cone keeps all the steam in, ensuring a very tender flavoursome dish). But these days a tagine can refer to almost any Moroccan stew whether it is cooked in the traditional dish or not.'

Navarin of Lamb Riblets

(SERVES 4–6)

1½ kg lamb riblets plain flour	Preheat oven to 180°C. Trim lamb well, removing most of the fat and sinew. Lightly flour them on both sides.
vegetable oil	Heat oil in a large heavy-bottomed pot. Brown riblets and remove.
2 large onions, chopped 3 garlic cloves, crushed	Add and sauté until soft (adding more oil if necessary).
800 g canned diced tomatoes, drained a little 2 cups beef stock, bought or homemade (see page 128) 8 baby potatoes, well scrubbed & halved 2–3 medium carrots, peeled & cut into thick slices freshly ground salt & pepper 2 bay leaves a few fresh thyme sprigs	Add, bring to the boil and return riblets. Mix well, cover and cook in oven for 1½ hours until meat is almost falling off bones.
1 cup frozen peas, thawed	Add and cook for 5 minutes. Then check seasoning.

'This is a dish which can only be eaten successfully with the fingers – so a large fingerbowl and plenty of napkins please. And for an even simpler dish, try brushing the trimmed riblets with mustard, then sprinkling with breadcrumbs and a little melted butter and roasting in the oven until golden, basting a few times.'

Lamb Shank Hotch Potch

(SERVES 6–8)

1.5 kg lamb shanks, French cut
$1/4$ cup vegetable oil

Heat oil in large heavy-bottomed pot and brown shanks in 2 or 3 lots. Set aside.

2 medium onions, chopped
3 celery stalks, diced
1 large swede, diced
3 medium carrots, diced

Add to pot and gently cook for 10 minutes.

chicken stock, bought or homemade
    (see page 62)
freshly ground salt & pepper

Return shanks to pot along with stock to cover. Gently simmer until shanks are tender (about $1^1/2$–2 hours). Remove shanks and set aside.

$1/2$ small cauliflower, cut into small flowerets
2 zucchini, diced

Add to liquid and cook for another 20 minutes. Then remove meat from shanks, dice and return to pot.

$1/4$ green cabbage, finely sliced
1 cup frozen green peas, thawed
2 tbsp chopped fresh parsley

Check seasoning, add cabbage, peas and parsley and boil for 5 minutes.

'A very popular recipe from my Scottish grandmother.'

Moussaka

(SERVES 6–8)

olive oil

2 onions, chopped

1 medium carrot, peeled & diced

2 celery stalks, diced

2 garlic cloves, crushed

Preheat oven to 210°C.
Heat a little oil in a large heavy-bottomed
pot and sauté vegies until lightly coloured.

1 kg lamb mince

Add and cook until it changes colour.

$^1/_2$ cup beef stock, bought or homemade
   (see page 128)

800 g canned tomato puree

$^1/_2$ cup dry white wine

1 tspn cinnamon

Tabasco, to taste

freshly ground salt & pepper

Add and mix well, breaking up any lumps
in the mince with a spoon. Gently simmer
for 20 minutes, adding more puree if
necessary.

3 medium eggplants, thickly sliced
olive oil
plain flour

3 tbsp butter
3 tbsp plain flour
2 cups hot milk
grated tasty cheese
freshly ground salt & pepper

extra grated tasty cheese

Heat a generous amount of oil in a pan and fry floured eggplant, in 3 or 4 lots, until golden. Drain well on paper towels.

In another pot, melt butter. Add flour, mix in well over a low heat and cook for a few minutes. Then add hot milk, whisking vigorously. Cook until thickish and smooth. Add a good handful of cheese and season to taste.

Lay half the eggplant in deep oven dish. Top with mince, rest of eggplant, then mornay sauce to cover. Generously sprinkle with cheese and cook in oven until golden and bubbling.

'If making the mornay sauce beforehand, stop a skin forming on the top by laying butter papers (or kitchen wrap) directly on top of the surface.'

Mini Lamb Roast with Potatoes, Garlic & Rosemary

(SERVES 4–6)

4 lamb mini roasts
olive oil

Preheat oven to its highest degree.
Trim lamb well. Then heat a little oil in a baking tray and brown on all sides.

12 baby potatoes, scrubbed & parboiled for
   10 minutes
1 garlic head broken into cloves, unpeeled
a few rosemary sprigs
freshly ground salt & pepper

Add, toss well and season.

Roast in oven for 15–20 minutes. Then rest lamb for a few minutes, before carving and serving with any juices poured over the top.

'You can, if you like, add some green herb butter (butter, chopped fresh herbs, a little garlic and lemon juice) to the roasting dish along with any of the juices and, once melted, pour over the top.'

South African Sosaties

(SERVES 4)

olive oil
2 medium onions, chopped

Heat a little oil in a pan and sauté onions until soft.

1 tspn ground coriander
$^1/_2$ tspn turmeric
1 tbsp Indian curry paste
1 garlic clove, crushed
juice of 2 limes
2 tbsp apricot jam
$^1/_4$ cup chicken stock, bought or homemade
   (see page 62)

Add, mix well and simmer for 5 minutes. Then cool.

2–3 lamb backstraps, trimmed well

Cut in 2–3 cm thick slices and refrigerate in marinade overnight.

1 large onion, cut in eighths and then in half
   crossways

Preheat BBQ or ridged grill.
Skewer lamb and onion and grill or BBQ, regularly brushing with marinade.

Rice Pilaf, optional (see page 105)
lime wedges

Serve with rice and lime wedges on the side.

'I know absolutely nothing about South African cooking. So, I must admit, I wouldn't have the faintest idea whether this is authentic or not.'

FURTHER THOUGHTS
on knives

★ Always buy the best — they are a lifetime investment. Any German or Swiss brands are invariably good. But whatever the brand, they should be heavy and solid and the blade should extend right through the handle to the end. (Blades that are not riveted in this way often come loose.)

★ Stainless steel knives are better for domestic use rather than carbon, which tend to rust if not immediately cleaned and dried after each use. And, whilst on that subject, all knives need to be rinsed and dried. They must not be thrown into the sink or dishwasher, where the blades can get damaged. In a similar vein, they shouldn't be just thrown into a drawer, but put in a knife bag, block or rack.

★ While it's nice to have a full set, this is not necessary for home use. You can, in most cases, get away with a 20 cm cook's knife, an 8-10 cm paring knife, a 20-25 cm thin carving knife and a steel.

★ And after use, always touch up your knives on the steel. Put the blade where it joins the handle at the tip of the steel and, at an angle of about 30°, bring the blade down the steel so that when it reaches the bottom you are sharpening the tip. Then repeat the process on the other side.

Roast Leg of Lamb, Greek Style

(SERVES 6–8)

1 cup red wine 1 tbsp chopped fresh rosemary 4 garlic cloves, crushed juice of 2 lemons	Combine.
1 leg of lamb	Pour marinade over lamb and refrigerate overnight, turning 2 or 3 times.
4 garlic cloves, crushed 1 tbsp chopped fresh rosemary olive oil lemon freshly ground salt & pepper	Preheat oven to 230°C. Mix garlic and rosemary together with olive oil and lemon juice to form a paste. Then make some cuts in lamb (about 2 cm deep) and massage paste all over and into slits. Put in a baking tray and season.
12–16 baby potatoes, well scrubbed	Put potatoes around meat, season and pour marinade in tray. Turn oven down to 180°C and roast for $1^3/_4$–2 hours basting regularly. Allow to rest for 10 minutes. Then slice and serve with pan juices over the top.

'A particularly stupid friend of mine got up twice in the middle of the night to turn the lamb over – I won't mention how ridiculous that is.'

Braised Lamb Shanks

(SERVES 4)

vegetable oil
8 lamb shanks, French cut
plain flour
freshly ground salt & pepper

Heat oil in a large heavy-bottomed pot. Flour shanks and, in two lots, brown on all sides. Remove and season.

2 onions, chopped
2 medium carrots, diced
2–3 celery stalks, diced
4 garlic cloves, crushed

Add a little more oil (if necessary) and sauté vegies until soft.

6 fresh thyme sprigs
3 tbsp balsamic vinegar
$^1\!/_2$ bottle dry white wine
2 pieces lemon peel

Add and boil until liquid is reduced by half.

800 g canned diced tomatoes, drained a little
2 bay leaves
1 cup beef stock, bought or homemade
   (see page 128)
2 tbsp chopped fresh parsley
freshly ground salt & pepper

Add, along with shanks, cover and gently simmer for about $1^1\!/_2$–2 hours until meat is very tender. Put in deep bowls.

gremolata, optional (see below)
creamy mash, optional (see page 156)

Sprinkle gremolata over the top and serve with mash.

'Gremolata (also known as gremolada) is traditionally sprinkled over the top of osso bucco. But it works well with almost any meat dish with a tomato flavoured sauce. To make it, simply mix together 4 tablespoons chopped fresh parsley, 1 tablespoon finely chopped garlic and 2 tablespoons each of finely chopped lemon and orange zest.'

Braised, Stuffed Forequarter of Lamb

(SERVES 6–8)

vegetable oil
1 medium carrot, peeled & finely diced
1 leek, well washed & finely diced
2 celery stalks, finely diced
1 large onion, finely chopped

Preheat oven to 150°C.
Heat a little oil in a pot and sauté vegies.
Put in a bowl.

250 g lamb mince
a good splash of soy sauce
1 egg
freshly ground salt & pepper

Add to bowl and mix in thoroughly.

1 forequarter of lamb, boned

Place on a bench, fat side down, and batten out. Then place stuffing lengthways along centre, roll and tie.

vegetable oil
1 medium carrot, peeled & diced
2 celery stalks, diced
1 large onion, chopped
1 leek, well washed & diced

Heat a little oil in a large, baking dish (with cover) and brown lamb on all sides. Remove, add vegies and sauté until soft.

3/4 cup chicken stock, bought or homemade
   (see page 62)
3/4 cup dry white wine
2 bay leaves

Add, mix well and return lamb. Cover and cook in oven for 2 hours or so, basting and turning regularly.

Crispy, Crunchy Roast Potatoes, optional
   (see page 246)

Remove lamb and reduce sauce if necessary. Slice lamb, place on plates and spoon sauce over the top.

'If you like, forget the stuffing and just season and roll the boned forequarter before continuing as above.'

Lancashire Hot Pot

(SERVES 4)

soft butter

Preheat oven to 180°C.
Butter bottom of a large casserole.

1 kg lamb neck chops
8 lamb kidneys, cleaned & halved (cores
    cut out)
6–8 large potatoes, sliced
3 large onions, sliced
3 medium carrots, sliced
freshly ground salt & pepper

Layer dish, starting and finishing with
potato and seasoning each layer well.

2 tspn chopped fresh thyme
2 cups beef stock, bought or homemade
    (see page 128)
soft butter

Sprinkle thyme over top, pour over stock
and dot with butter. Bake, covered, for
2 hours. Then remove lid and cook for
another 30 minutes.

'This is not my mother's recipe, but hot pot was a popular
dish in my youth – so much so that if you bought neck chops
from the local butcher he would invariably ask whether you
were making a hot pot.'

Barbecued Rump of Beef with Charred Onion Salad

(SERVES 8–10)

8 brown onions, skin on & halved	Preheat covered BBQ. Place onions, flesh side down, around the edges of a lightly oiled grill and cook, regularly turning.
1 cup olive oil 1 tbsp Dijon mustard a good splash of soy sauce 1 heaped tspn sambal oelek	Whisk together.
1 whole rump, trimmed well	Put in centre of BBQ, generously paint with oil mix, cover and cook for about 40 minutes (for medium-rare), brushing and turning regularly. Remove and rest for 10 minutes before slicing.
extra virgin olive oil red wine vinegar freshly ground salt & pepper chopped fresh parsley	To make salad, slip onions from skin and dress to taste with oil, vinegar, seasonings and parsley. Slice beef, pour any juices over the top and serve with the salad on the side.

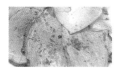

'A BBQ is not just about snags, steaks and chops – you can also whip up classy dinner or lunch party fare by using large joints of meat as in this case.'

Mustard-Crusted Fillet of Beef with Minted Green Pea Puree

(SERVES 4)

600 g piece of eye fillet of beef, trimmed well
freshly ground salt & pepper
Dijon mustard

Preheat oven to its highest temperature. Place beef in a roasting tray, season and generously smear with mustard. For medium-rare, cook for about 20 minutes. (If you want to cook more, turn heat down to 200°C once beef goes in.) When cooked, remove and set beef aside to rest for 5–10 minutes.

4 cups frozen peas, thawed
8 fresh mint sprigs
salt

While beef is resting, put in boiling water. When water comes back to the boil, drain.

a good dollop of butter
a splash of cream
freshly ground salt & pepper

Whiz peas up in blender or processor with butter and cream. Season to taste and mound on plates. Thickly slice beef and put a couple of slices on top along with any juices.

'In season (October–December) use fresh green peas, but cook for 5–10 minutes before pureeing.'

Steak Sandwich with Pesto

(SERVES 4)

basil pesto, bought or homemade
  (see page 42)
1 baguette

Preheat ridged grill and oven to 200°C. Slice baguette in half lengthways, smear inside generously with pesto, re-form and wrap in foil. Cook in oven for 8–10 minutes.

4 x 100 g porterhouse steaks, trimmed of
  all fat & sinew
2–3 ripe tomatoes, cut in thick slices
1 red onion, sliced

When almost ready, batten out steaks and cook to desired degree on oiled grill along with the tomatoes and onion (or panfry them).

cos lettuce leaves
mayonnaise, bought or homemade
  (see page 23), mixed with pesto to taste

Lay baguette base on a bench and top with lettuce, tomato, onion and steak. Sprinkle with mayo, press lid on and cut into 4 crossways.

Sybil's Cabbage & Gherkin Slaw, optional
  (see page 231)

Serve with a generous amount of slaw on the side.

'What has happened to steak sangas? I remember when every pub served terrific versions between thick slabs of bread with lots of fried onion, crisp lettuce and a good slab of beef – the less said about the current efforts the better (that is, if you can find a pub which is not trendified and actually serves the blessed things).'

A Classic Pepper Steak with Sautéed Potatoes

(SERVES 2)

6–8 baby potatoes, well scrubbed
table salt

Cook in salted water until almost tender. Drain well.

olive oil
freshly ground salt

Heat a generous amount of oil in a stainless steel pan. Cut potatoes in half crossways and put cut side down in pan. Cook over moderate heat until golden on all sides. Drain well on paper towels and salt to taste. (Keep hot, if necessary, in the oven.)

olive oil
2 x 180 g fillet steaks, trimmed of all
   fat & sinew
freshly ground salt & pepper

At the same time, heat a little oil in another pan and seal steaks all over. Remove and season.

a good dollop of butter
$^1/_2$ medium onion, finely chopped
2 tbsp brandy
$^1/_2$ cup beef stock, bought or homemade
   (see page 128)
$^1/_4$ cup thickened cream
1 tbsp drained green peppercorns
1 tbsp chopped fresh parsley
1 tbsp Dijon mustard

Pour off most of oil, add butter and onion and sauté until soft. Then add rest of ingredients, mix well and simmer for 3–4 minutes. Return beef and cook to desired degree, turning once or twice and basting regularly (don't boil). Serve with sautéed potatoes on the side.

'In my early days in the kitchen, I cooked about 4 million pepper steaks. I still think it's a pretty terrific dish which maybe deserves another 15 minutes of fame.'

FURTHER THOUGHTS
on the cooking of steaks

★ The most important point of all — the steak itself. The cut of meat is up to you (although if you have had problems with tenderness, fillet is almost failsafe). But no matter which cut you choose, your steak must be thick, cut in even slices and trimmed of most fat and sinew.

★ To me, there are only three ways to cook a steak (although I have come up with a rather tricky fourth way — see below). If the weather is fine — on the Barbie. And if not, on a ridged grill or in a heavy-bottomed cast iron pan. And, in each case, get them very hot before adding either oil or the steak itself.

★ Once you slap the steak on the grill, barbie or whatever, always leave it for 2 or 3 minutes before moving (to develop the crust), only ever turn it 2 or 3 times and never, ever season it until it is sealed (salt draws out the juices).

★ To check when it is ready, prod it with your finger. Rare steak is decidedly soft to the touch, medium has a firm bounce and anything over that begins to feel tight and hard.

★ And, last but not least, if your steak cooking endeavours are less than perfect, try this cheats method. Preheat the oven to its highest degree, spread a layer of rock salt on an oven tray and cook in oven until it begins to crackle. Then place steak on top and cook until desired degree, only turning once (and placing back on a fresh area of salt).

Two Minute Steak with Date Salad

(SERVES 4)

4 x 150 g porterhouse steaks, trimmed of all fat & sinew	Preheat grill or BBQ. Batten out a little.
1 heaped tbsp chopped fresh mint 1 heaped tbsp chopped fresh coriander 1 heaped tbsp chopped fresh parsley juice of 1 lemon 1 tbsp green Tabasco a splash of soy sauce 1 tbsp honey 4 tbsp olive oil	Whisk together, set half aside and brush the rest over steaks. Leave for 10 minutes.
1/2 red onion, finely sliced 1/4 continental (telegraph) cucumber, sliced 8 cherry tomatoes, halved 4 large pitted green olives, sliced 8 dates, sliced a small handful of Italian (flat leaf) parsley sprigs	Toss with reserved marinade. Then cook steaks to desired degree, brushing with marinade as you do so. Serve with a mound of salad.

'How to cook a steak at the pub barbie – as told to Gay Bilson by a cockie from the bush! You throw it on the barbie and slowly drink a beer. Go back to the barbie, turn it, then drink another beer. When you have finished the second beer the steak is done – sounds fair enough to me.'

T-Bones with Chimichurri Sauce

(SERVES 4)

6 garlic cloves, chopped
4 spring (green) onions, chopped
3 tbsp chopped fresh parsley
1 tbsp chopped fresh oregano
1 heaped tspn sambal oelek
1 heaped tspn mustard
a splash of soy sauce
4 tbsp red wine vinegar
freshly ground pepper
3/4 cup olive oil

Preheat oven to its highest degree.
Whiz up and set aside for 30 minutes to
develop flavours.

olive oil
4 x 300 g thick T-bone steaks
freshly ground salt

Smear steaks with a little of the sauce.
Then seal over a high heat in an oiled pan.
Season with salt once sealed and smear with
more sauce. Cook in oven to desired
degree, turning once and smearing with
more sauce 2 or 3 times.

24–36 green beans, topped & tailed
table salt

Cook beans in a large pot of lightly salted
boiling water until crisp-tender. Then drain
well. Serve steaks on a bed of beans with
extra sauce drizzled over the top.

'Chimichurri is an Argentinian garlicky staple which comes in many
forms including relish style where lots of diced, blanched corn, tomatoes
and capsicum are added (but please note that the amount of garlic
is compulsory).'

Fillet Steak with Blackbeans & Snowpeas

(SERVES 4)

4 x 200 g thick fillet steaks, trimmed of all fat & sinew
½ cup Chinese wine
4 tbsp oyster sauce
2 tbsp kecap manis
1 tbsp Asian fish sauce
1 tspn sesame oil

Put steak in a bowl, combine liquid ingredients and pour over the top. Refrigerate overnight, turning 2 or 3 times.

2 tbsp blackbeans

Soak in water for 20 minutes. Drain, rinse well and drain again. Then mash with a fork.

peanut oil
2 garlic cloves, crushed

Heat a little oil in a pan and sauté garlic. Then add steak and seal on both sides. Remove and set aside.

½ cup water

Add marinating liquid to pan along with blackbeans and water. Simmer for a few minutes. Then return steaks to pan and gently cook to desired degree, basting and turning regularly.

table salt
24 snowpeas, topped & tailed

Briefly blanch in lots of lightly salted boiling water. Drain well and place on plates. Top with steaks and pour sauce over the top.

'I'm not absolutely sure where this ripper recipe comes from, but I think it may be from that very exciting Sydney chef, Kylie Kwong.'

Beef Stock

(MAKES 3 LITRES)

4 kg veal or small beef bones including knuckles & marrow bones (ask your butcher to chop bones into 10 cm pieces)
1 kg beef brisket
100 g ghee
100 g honey

Preheat oven to 200°C.
Coarsely chop brisket and put in a large roasting tray with bones. Melt ghee and honey, brush all over and cook in oven until lightly browned. Then put in a stock pot.

3 large carrots, unpeeled & chopped
4 leeks, washed & chopped
2 celery stalks, chopped
a handful of mushroom peelings & stalks
6 garlic cloves, chopped
1 bottle dry white wine

Add vegies to the roasting tray and sauté until lightly brown. Then add wine and reduce until almost evaporated. Add to stock pot.

2 large onions, skin on & halved

Cook onions, skin side down, until dark brown. Then add to pot along with cold water to about 10 cm above contents. Bring to the boil then simmer very gently, regularly skimming, for 30 minutes.

parsley stalks
2 bay leaves
12 whole black peppercorns
800 g canned diced tomatoes, drained

Add to pot and simmer for 4–5 hours, adding more water if bones become exposed. Strain, cool and refrigerate overnight. Next day, remove the layer of fat.

'A stock that is made with garbage will taste like garbage.'
Famed chef, Alice Waters

Greek Beef Stew

(SERVES 6–8)

olive oil

1 kg stewing steak, trimmed well & cut in
   largish cubes

plain flour

freshly ground salt & pepper

Heat a thin layer of oil in a large heavy-bottomed pot. Flour beef and brown, in two or three lots. Remove, season and set aside.

olive oil

2 medium onions, chopped

1 large carrot, peeled & diced

2 celery stalks, diced

4 garlic cloves, crushed

Add a little more oil if necessary, and gently sauté vegies.

$1^1/_2$ cups red wine

$1^1/_2$ cups beef stock, bought or homemade
   (see page 128)

1 tspn allspice

2 tbsp balsamic vinegar

800 g canned diced tomatoes, drained a little

8 baby potatoes, scrubbed & quartered

freshly ground salt & pepper

Add, mix well and bring to the boil. Return beef, cover, turn heat down and simmer very gently for 2 hours (adding more liquid if necessary). Serve with steamed broccoli and/or green beans.

'The biggest mistake people make when whipping up a stew is cutting the meat too small (by the time the sauce is thick and fragrant, the meat is overcooked). So, no smaller than $1^1/_2$ cm cubes.'

Lamb's Fry with Onions & Sage

(SERVES 2–4)

olive oil
a knob of butter

Heat a few tablespoons of oil and butter in a pan.

2 onions, sliced
1 garlic clove, crushed
$1/2$ cup chicken stock, bought or homemade (see page 62)
$1/4$ cup dry white wine

Add and gently cook for 12–15 minutes until most of the liquid has disappeared and onion is tender.

a good splash of balsamic vinegar
freshly ground salt & pepper

Add, mix well and set aside. Keep warm.

plain flour
1 tbsp chopped fresh parsley
olive oil
6–8 thickish slices of lamb's liver (fry)

Mix parsley and flour. Lightly flour liver. In a non-stick pan, heat a thin layer of oil until almost smoking and sear in two lots, until crusty on the outside and pink within.

2 tbsp butter
4–8 sage leaves

Put a mound of onion on each plate and top with lamb's fry. Then put butter and sage into pan and fry leaves until crisp. Put sage on top of liver and pour pan juices over the top.

'I have always been intrigued by lamb's fry — why is it not just called liver? Perhaps it's an attempt to make it sound more palatable(in a similar vein to sweetbreads, or variety meats, as offal is known in the States). Or is the name derived simply from the fact that it is commonly fried?'

Steak & Kidney Pie

(SERVES 6–8)

plain flour olive oil 1 kg stewing steak, trimmed well & cubed freshly ground salt & pepper	Lightly flour beef. Heat a thin layer of oil in a large heavy-bottomed pot and seal in two or three lots. Remove, season and set aside.
olive oil 2 large onions, chopped 2 garlic cloves, crushed	Add more oil, if necessary, and sauté vegies until golden.
3 tbsp plain flour	Return beef and add flour. Mix well and gently cook for 3–4 minutes.
$^1/_2$ cup port	Add and reduce by half.
2 cups beef stock, bought or homemade (see page 128) 6–8 lamb's kidneys, cleaned & cut into 6	Add, mix in well and simmer very gently for $1^1/_2$ hours. Cool a little.
1 sheet of puff pastry 1 egg a little milk	Preheat oven to 210°C. Place beef in a deep ovenproof dish, top with pastry and trim edges. Then beat egg and milk together and brush over the top. Bake in oven for about 30 minutes until hot and golden.

'Some more useless information. In Cockney rhyming slang, Steak and Kidney Pie is known as 'Kate and Sidney Pie'. And the pie itself first came to prominence when Mrs Beeton, listed a recipe for it in 1861.'

Pot au Feu of Tongue

(SERVES 6–8)

2 ox tongues, brined for 24 hours
chicken or beef stock, bought or homemade
   (see page 62 or 128)
1 large carrot, peeled & sliced
1 medium onion, sliced
2 garlic cloves, crushed
1 tspn whole black peppercorns
6 parley sprigs

Put in a pressure cooker and just cover with stock. Bring to pressure and cook for 20 minutes. Then depressurise and strain. Return tongues and stock to cooker.

$1/2$ green cabbage, core in
12 baby potatoes, scrubbed
2 whole medium carrots, peeled
2 whole medium leeks, well washed

Add, bring back to pressure and cook for another 10 minutes. Depressurise cooker, peel tongue and cut into thick slices. Then cut cabbage into wedges and carrots and leeks into slices.

1 tbsp Dijon mustard
1 tbsp chopped fresh herbs
6 tbsp mayonnaise, bought or homemade
   (see page 23)

Mix.
Share tongue and vegies amongst bowls, sprinkle with stock and serve with Dijon mustard mayonnaise.

'I remember when it was suggested that for **Healthy, Wealthy & Wise** I whip up some recipes using the pressure cooker. I must admit that I approached the idea with a certain amount of trepidation because of childhood memories of loud explosions, food decorated walls and lots of cursing. But I can now report that, thankfully, pressure cooker technology has improved dramatically and they are an asset in any kitchen.'

Corned Beef with Mustard Sauce

(SERVES 6–8)

1 x 1 kg piece of corned silverside

Place in a pot, cover with cold water and bring to a gentle boil. Discard water, rinse both meat and pot and cover with fresh, cold water.

1 large onion, quartered
1 large carrot, quartered
1/4 cup white vinegar
1 tspn mustard seeds
6 whole cloves
2 whole garlic cloves
1 tbsp brown sugar

Add, bring to the boil and simmer very gently for about $1-1^1/4$ hours (putting a plate on top of the beef to keep it submerged).

vegetable oil
1 large onion, finely chopped
$1^1/2$ cups beef stock, bought or homemade
   (see page 128)
$^1/2$ cup fresh tomato puree
2 tbsp Dijon mustard

Heat a little oil in a pot and sauté onion until soft. Then add rest of ingredients and simmer until thickish. Set aside. When corned beef is ready, turn heat off and add some strained stock to sauce. Bring to the boil and cook for 3–4 minutes.

$^1/2$–1 small green cabbage, cored & cut into
   6–8 wedges
18–24 baby carrots, peeled

Cook in a large pot of boiling water until just tender. Drain well, and then slice corned beef and serve with vegies and sauce.

'If you have leftovers, make corned beef hash. Just boil some potatoes (and sweet spuds if you like) and coarsely mash. To that, add some sautéed sliced onions and cabbage along with cubed corned beef. Form into patties, lightly flour and cook. Serve with a fried egg on the top.'

Hi
Hewy – Baby!

We have been watching your program 'Huey's Cooking Adventures' for sometime now but have become increasingly disappointed in its content. I am sure (well, pretty sure) that most of your watchers are not as diet conscious as you think. Most of your recipes are either Asian or for fatties! Give us some Aussie food that most of us were brought up on, but with an expert cook's innovative flair – yes, we do think you have it!
Get your act together Huey!
Pat & Pat QLD

I would like to know how you have slimmed down as you're looking better and more handsomer week by week. What do you have for breakfast, lunch and dinner? I personally think you should bring out a recipe book for people who want to lose weight.
Rose NSW

I politely write to you to ask your diagnosis. Being an MMB (Mere Male Bachelor), one is always looking for help in improving cooking methods. I love curried sausages, but I get reactions from over spicing. Garlic is a no-no; chilli can be the same. Could you please suggest an appropriate course of treatment?
John QLD

Spice-Rubbed Rib Eye of Beef

(SERVES 8–10)

1 cup olive oil
3 garlic cloves, crushed
3 tspn paprika
4 tspn yellow mustard seeds
$1/2$ tspn cayenne
freshly ground salt & pepper
1 tspn brown sugar
a splash of soy
1 tspn sambal oelek

Preheat a covered BBQ.
Whisk together in a bowl.

rosemary stalks
1 x 2 kg whole rib eye of beef, well trimmed

Throw rosemary on top of coals.
Generously paint beef with spice mix and
put on oiled grill. Cook to desired degree,
regularly brushing with spice mix (a meat
thermometer is a good idea).

BBQ Potatoes with Lemon & Chive Dressing,
  optional (see page 24)

Allow to rest for 10 minutes. Then slice and
serve with juices poured over the top and
potatoes on the side.

'If inviting a larger group to a barbie forget the steaks
and chops and instead think slabs of meat, such as this
whole rib eye or a butterflied leg of lamb. It not only
makes life a lot easier, but the end result is perfectly cooked, juicy meat.
(If, like me, you prefer your meat rare, simply cook it that way. Then whack
some sliced meat back on to the barbie for those who prefer it more done).'

Shin of Veal in Red Wine with Crushed Potatoes

(SERVES 4)

olive oil
1 x 750 g piece of veal shin
plain flour
freshly ground salt & pepper

Heat a little oil in a large, heavy-bottomed pot. Flour meat and brown on all sides. Season and set aside.

olive oil
1 large onion, chopped
1 large carrot, peeled & diced
2 celery stalks, diced
2 garlic cloves, crushed
1 tbsp fresh rosemary needles

Add extra oil, if necessary, and sauté vegies until soft.

2 tbsp plain flour

Add, mix well and gently cook for 3–4 minutes, continually stirring.

$1^{1}/_{2}$ cups red wine
1 cup beef stock, bought or homemade (see page 128)
400–800 g canned diced tomatoes, drained a little
$^{1}/_{4}$ cup extra dry vermouth
freshly ground salt & pepper

Add and bring to the boil. Return veal to pot, cover, and simmer very gently for $1^{1}/_{2}$–$1^{3}/_{4}$ hours until meat is almost falling off the bone, turning and basting regularly and adding more stock if necessary.

8–12 baby potatoes, well scrubbed
olive oil
8 pitted black olives, chopped
8 basil leaves, chopped fresh
a squeeze of fresh lemon juice

When veal is ready, cook spuds until tender. Then drain well and crush roughly with a fork. Mix in rest of ingredients and season to taste. Mound on plates, pull veal off bone and put large chunks on top. Pour sauce over the lot.

'You could also make this in the style of osso bucco, with sliced shin, rather than the whole piece.'

Baby Veal Cutlets with Microwave Blue Cheese Polenta

(SERVES 4)

4 baby veal cutlets, well trimmed
olive oil
2 tspn fresh rosemary needles
lemon juice

Preheat oven to 200°C.
Place cutlets on a plate, sprinkle with oil, rosemary and lemon juice. Turn to coat a few times and leave for 15–20 minutes.

3 cups water
1 cup polenta
2 tspn rock salt

Put in a microwave-safe bowl and cook, uncovered, at 100% for 6 minutes. Stir well, cover loosely with greaseproof paper and cook for a further 6 minutes.

2 dollops of butter
50 g soft blue cheese, chopped
freshly ground salt & pepper

Add to polenta and mix well.

olive oil
freshly ground salt & pepper

While polenta is cooking, heat a little oil in a pan which can go into the oven and seal veal on both sides. Season, pour over marinade and cook in oven, turning once, until firmish (not hard) when pressed with a finger.

To serve, mound polenta on plates, top with cutlets and pour any juices over the top.

'Another very popular recipe. I think this may have had something to do with this very easy way to successfully cook polenta.'

HUEY'S
TOP TEN

Kitchen Bits & Pieces

★ Rice cooker — I don't know how I ever did without one, particularly since I've discovered variations on the simple steamed rice theme.

★ A sauté pan with straight sides and a tight-fitting lid to enable more food to be cooked gently and evenly in one layer.

★ The microplane grater — what started as a woodworking tool is now the perfect piece of equipment to grate everything from ginger, garlic and lemongrass to citrus zest, cheese and chocolate.

★ A ridged grill — so that I can BBQ inside when it's snowing out (or when I just can't be bothered firing up the beast).

★ The best knives — absolutely essential.

★ A manual coffee grinder — I use one for grinding spices (or two because they make great pepper grinders too).

★ And while on that subject — good pepper and salt grinders.

★ A set of heavy-bottomed, stainless steel pots (including an extra large stockpot) — make sure they have good solid handles.

★ A wok with a flattened bottom — this makes it more suitable for domestic use.

★ And, of course, lots of tea towels — to put in my back pocket.

Parmentier's Hash

(SERVES 4–6)

olive oil
2 medium onions, chopped
2 celery stalks, diced
1 medium carrot, diced
2 bacon rashers, diced
1 garlic clove, crushed

Preheat oven to 220°C.
Heat a little oil in a heavy-bottomed pot and sauté vegies until soft.

1 kg stewing steak, trimmed well & cubed

Add and cook until sealed.

3 tbsp plain flour

Add flour, turn heat down and cook for 3–4 minutes.

3 cups beef stock, bought or homemade (see page 128)
800 g canned diced tomatoes, drained
freshly ground salt & pepper
a splash of worcestershire

Add and simmer for about $1^1/_2$ hours until thick and fragrant. Cool a little.

creamy mash (see page 156) using 6 large potatoes
grated tasty cheese

Spread a layer of mash in a deep oven dish. Top with beef mix and then top with rest of mash and plenty of grated cheese. Bake for 20–25 minutes until golden and bubbling.

'A traditional French dish which is not far removed from our shepherd's or cottage pie. It is named after, as are many French potato based dishes, the man who introduced the potato to the French Court of Louis XVI (he even, as a publicity gimmick, persuaded the Queen, Marie Antoinette, to wear potato flowers as an ornament).'

Beef Chili with Beer

(SERVES 4–6)

olive oil 1 large onion, finely chopped 3–4 garlic cloves, sliced 2 chillies, chopped	Heat a little oil in a large heavy-bottomed pot and sauté.
1 tbsp dried oregano 1 tspn ground cumin 1 tspn ground cinnamon 2 tbsp chilli powder (Mexican preferably) 2 tbsp cocoa powder	Add and toss for 1–2 minutes.
600 g lean beef mince	Add and cook, breaking lumps up with a spoon, until it changes colour.
300 ml beer 1 cup water 800 g canned diced tomatoes, drained freshly ground salt & pepper 1 tbsp chopped parsley	Add and bring to the boil. Then gently simmer for 1–1$^1/_4$ hours until rich and thick (adding more liquid if necessary).
480 g canned red kidney beans, well drained & rinsed	Add, mix well and cook for 5 minutes.
sour cream grated tasty cheese 2 spring (green) onions, chopped	Put in bowls and top with sour cream, cheese and spring onion.

'In the States they have a grind of mince called chili grind. It is coarser than normal mince and, to my mind, works a little better. So, if possible ask your butcher to mince the stewing steak more coarsely than normal.'

Moroccan Keftas in Tomato & Preserved Lemon Sauce

(SERVES 6–8)

olive oil
2 medium onions, finely chopped
4 garlic cloves, crushed

Heat a little oil in a heavy-bottomed pot and sauté until soft. Remove half and set aside.

800 g canned diced tomatoes, drained a little
1 tspn ground coriander
$^1/_2$ tspn ground cumin
1 tspn sambal oelek
$^1/_2$ tspn garam masala
1 good tbsp honey
$^1/_2$ cup chicken stock, bought or homemade (see page 62)
2 pieces sliced preserved lemon, bought or homemade (see page 226)

Add to pot and gently cook for 10 minutes.

800 g lean minced lamb
$^1/_3$ cup yoghurt
$^1/_2$ tbsp sambal oelek
$^1/_2$ tbsp sweet paprika
$^1/_2$ tbsp ground cumin
3 tbsp chopped fresh coriander

Mix in bowl with reserved onion and garlic. With wet hands, form into meatballs and cook in a lightly oiled pan until sealed all over. Add to sauce and cook, gently, turning regularly for another 10 minutes or so.

2 tbsp chopped fresh coriander

Mix in.

'These can be served with either couscous (see page 248) or Lemon Rice (see page 233) and, if you're going the whole hog, the Moroccan Salad (see page 20) and a pot of Mint Tea (see page 224).'

American Meatball Sandwich

(SERVES 4)

olive oil 1 small fennel bulb, finely chopped $\frac{1}{2}$ large onion, finely chopped 2 garlic cloves, crushed $\frac{1}{2}$ tspn ground coriander $\frac{1}{2}$ tspn ground cumin 1 tspn sambal oelek	Heat a little oil in a pan and sauté vegies until soft. Then add spices and sambal and toss for 1–2 minutes.
250 g lean beef mince 250 g pork mince 1 egg 2 tbsp breadcrumbs 2 tbsp chopped fresh parsley freshly ground salt & pepper	Add and mix well.
plain flour	Form into 12 patties, lightly flour and panfry until golden in two or three lots. Drain well on paper towels.
tomato based pasta sauce 1 baguette a small handful baby rocket 2 roasted red capsicum, sliced	While patties are cooking, heat pasta sauce. Cut bread in half lengthways and then generously brush sauce on base. Then top with rocket, meatballs and capsicum, and press top on firmly. Cut into 4 crossways.

'To roast capsicum, cut tops and bottoms off and remove cores and seeds. Then place on a baking tray, skin side up, and either cook in a very hot oven or under an overhead grill until blistered and brown – black. Cover with a towel and allow to cool. Then peel and slice.'

All American Meatloaf

(SERVES 6–8)

olive oil
1 medium red onion, chopped
1 green capsicum, diced
2 garlic cloves, crushed

Preheat oven to 220°C.
Heat a little oil in a pan and sauté vegies
until softish.

2 thick slices country-style bread
beef stock, bought or homemade
  (see page 128)

Soak bread in stock until moist. Then
squeeze out excess liquid and put in a
bowl along with vegies.

2 large eggs
1 kg lean beef mince
3 tbsp chopped fresh parsley
3/4 cup BBQ sauce
2 tbsp Dijon mustard
freshly ground salt & pepper

Add and mix well.

melted butter

Lightly butter a loaf tin or deep oven dish
and put in meat mix. Press into corners
and cook in oven for 1¼ hours.

BBQ sauce
creamy mash (see page 156)

Remove from oven, lightly brush with
BBQ sauce and leave for 10 minutes, before
slicing and serving with mash.

'One of my favourite TV programs was **Happy Days** (although it was never as good after Ritchie and Ralph Mouth left). But that aside, because meatloaf was the favourite of the whole family, I felt I should investigate this American classic — and was surprised by how good it was (particularly in sandwiches with a good dollop of chutney).'

Pork Chops with Apples & Dry Apple Cider Glaze

(SERVES 4)

olive oil
4 thickish midloin pork chops

Preheat oven to 180°C.
Heat a little oil in a pan and, over a moderate heat, cook pork for about 5 minutes until well browned on both sides.

4 Granny Smith apples, peeled, cored & sliced
2 tbsp honey
juice of $\frac{1}{2}$ lemon
ground cinnamon
$\frac{1}{4}$ cup chicken stock, bought or homemade (see page 62)

Scatter apples over base of a baking tray and sprinkle with honey, lemon juice and a little cinnamon. Top with pork chops and pour stock around the side. Tightly cover with foil and cook in oven for 35–40 minutes until chops are tender.

$\frac{1}{2}$ cup chicken stock, bought or homemade (see page 62)
$\frac{1}{2}$ cup apple juice
$\frac{1}{4}$ cup dry apple cider
2 tbsp calvados
2 tbsp soy sauce
1 tbsp balsamic vinegar

At the same time, put in a small pot and reduce to a glaze, adding any cooking juices towards the end. To serve, place apples on plates, top with pork and pour glaze over the top.

'Calvados is an apple brandy from the Normandy region in France (a region which also has the most delicious pork, purely and simply because the pigs are fed on apples). If you don't happen to have a bottle in the cellar, a splash of normal brandy will do almost as well.'

Rack of Pork with Roasted Pears

(SERVES 6)

1 x 6 chop rack of pork, with rind finely scored
table salt
olive oil
chicken stock, bought or homemade
  (see page 62)

Preheat oven to 210°C.
Rub pork rind with salt and oil and cook in oven for 20 minutes. Then turn temperature down to 170°C and cook for 1 hour, adding small amounts of stock to pan every 10 minutes or so. Remove pork and rest for 10 minutes.

6 pears
olive oil

About 30 minutes before pork is ready, rub pears with olive oil and put in a separate tray in oven.

1 garlic clove, crushed
juice of ½ lemon
a good dollop of butter

While pork is resting, strain pan juices into a pot. Add garlic and lemon juice and boil to reduce. (if necessary, add some extra stock at this stage.) When a light glaze is formed, add butter and swirl to incorporate.

Cut pork into chops and serve with pears and a drizzle of sauce over the top.

'One of my favourites from my childhood goes well with this – carrot and parsnip mash. Just boil equal quantities of carrots and parsnips until tender. Then coarsely mash with seasonings and a good dollop of butter.'

Japanese Braised Pork Fillet

(SERVES 4)

2–3 pork fillets, trimmed well & cut into
    2 cm cubes
1 tbsp sake
4 tbsp cornflour

Place pork in a bowl. Toss with sake and then cornflour.

6 cups vegetable oil

Heat in a wok to about 180°C and fry pork in two or three lots until crispy. Drain well on paper towels.

6 tbsp Japanese soy sauce
6 tbsp pear juice
1 tbsp molasses
1 tbsp caster sugar
1 tspn freshly grated ginger
3 garlic cloves, crushed
2 spring (green) onions, chopped
1 tbsp sesame oil
$^{1}/_{4}$ cup water

Bring to the boil, add pork and gently simmer until a light glaze is formed.

12 small snowpeas, halved
steamed rice

Add snowpeas and toss for a minute or so. Serve on rice.

'This is not a braise in the true sense of the word, which is why I use a premium cut of pork which only needs a short period of cooking. (To eke it out, you can add other vegies, such as sweet potatoes or even some other Asian greens at the last moment.'

BBQ Baby Back Ribs with Coca-Cola Sauce

(SERVES 4)

2 cups Coca-Cola

1 cup tomato sauce

$^1/_4$ cup Thai sweet chilli sauce

2 tbsp red wine vinegar

2 tbsp Worcestershire

2 garlic cloves, crushed

1 tspn sambal oelek

freshly ground pepper

Preheat a kettle BBQ.

Simmer in a pot for 20 minutes.

4 slabs baby back pork ribs

Generously brush with sauce and cook over a moderate heat for 35–40 minutes, regularly brushing.

4 large potatoes, salted & wrapped in foil

sour cream

At the same time, cook potatoes and when ready cut a cross in the top and add a dollop of sour cream.

'This sauce is derived from one of the Weber BBQ cookbooks and, although it sounds a little weird, it is actually delicious and works brilliantly with any barbecued pork.'

FURTHER THOUGHTS
on keeping pork juicy & tender

★ Because pork is mostly now bred lean and mean it can be dry. So, at the risk of repeating myself, it is important not to over cook it. Forget that old wives' tale about pork being dangerous unless it is cooked within an inch of its life — trichinosis, which to my knowledge has never been found in Australia, is negated by the pork being medium. So a little pink in the centre please — you will be surprised by the difference.

★ A brine is an old fashioned way of tenderising pork. Try it because it does work. Just whisk together 2 cups each of water and lager, $\frac{1}{4}$ cup rock salt, 1 cup ice cubes, 3 tablespoons of raw sugar and 2 tablespoons of molasses. Then immerse the pork in the mix and refrigerate for 24 hours.

★ And, of course, let us not forget a simple marinade. Start with a basic little oil, lemon juice and garlic number and add your own variations such as honey, soy, sambal oelek, curry paste, fresh herbs, etc.

★ The Americans, who think that a barbecue is hardly a barbecue unless pork features in one form or other, often use dry rubs instead of marinades. Try this all rounder — mix 1 teaspoon each of mustard powder, onion powder, paprika and freshly ground salt with $\frac{1}{2}$ teaspoon each of garlic powder, ground coriander, ground cumin and freshly ground pepper. Then rub it into the pork and leave for 1 hour.

Pork Chops with Macaroni & Corn Cheese

(SERVES 4)

4 thickish pork chops brine (see page 150)	Put pork in brine and refrigerate for 24 hours.
300–400 g macaroni table salt 2–3 corn cobs, kernels removed olive oil	Preheat oven to 210°C. Cook macaroni in plenty of lightly salted boiling water until al dente, adding corn for the last minute. Drain well and toss with a little oil. Then remove chops from brine, drain well and pat dry. Pan fry in a little oil to seal on both sides and then cook in oven for 10–12 minutes until cooked. (Don't over cook – to check if cooked, make a small cut.)
2 cups mornay sauce (see page 86) 1 heaped tbsp mascarpone 2 tbsp freshly grated parmesan 1 tbsp chopped fresh parsley	At the same time, heat mornay and add cheese, pasta and parsley. Place in bowls and top with chops.

 'Pigs, because they did not survive on foods such as grass and leaves (and in fact competed with humans for foods such as grains and nuts), were one of the last species to be domesticated. That was not until 2200 BC when the Chinese discovered that it was these eating habits which made pork taste so sweet.'

Roast Pork with Crispy Crackling & Apple Gravy

(SERVES 6–8)

4 kg leg of pork, rind finely scored
table salt
olive oil
1 onion, roughly chopped
chicken stock, bought or homemade
   (see page 62)

Preheat oven to 200°C.
Rub rind thoroughly with salt and oil. Put onion along with a little stock in a roasting tray and put pork on a rack on top. Cook for 30 minutes, then turn heat down to 180°C. Cook for about 20 minutes per 500 g, adding more stock if necessary. When ready, remove pork and rest for 10 minutes.

6 Granny Smith apples, peeled, cored & cut
   into eighths
1 tspn sugar
a good pinch of cinnamon
chicken stock, as above

While meat is cooking, boil until tender in a little stock.

a heaped tbsp plain flour
2–3 cups chicken stock, as above, hot
freshly ground salt & pepper
roasted vegetables

To make gravy discard onion and spoon off most of the fat from the tray (leaving 2 tablespoons behind). Using a wooden spoon, scrape up all the brown bits from tray. Then add flour and cook for 1–2 minutes over a low heat. Add stock, bit by bit, continually whisking. Strain into a pot and add apple, along with more stock if necessary. Season to taste. Carve pork and serve with gravy and plenty of roasted vegies which have been cooked in a separate tray.

'There is no great secret to crispy crackling. Just ensure that your butcher scores the rind finely (about 1 cm apart) and generously rub it with table salt and oil before starting off in a fairly hot oven. And, don't ever cover it with foil as this will make the skin soft.'

Bacon, Egg & Tomato Pie

(SERVES 6–8)

vegetable oil
6 lean bacon rashers, sliced
3 medium onions, sliced

Preheat oven to 200°C.
Heat a little oil in a pan and sauté until soft.

8 eggs
4 large tomatoes, cored & thickly sliced
freshly ground salt & pepper

Spread half of above mix in a deep oven dish. Make 4 wells (evenly spaced) and break in 4 eggs. Season and lay half of tomatoes on top. Then repeat process with bacon mix, eggs and the rest of tomatoes.

1 frozen puff pastry sheet
1 egg
3 tbsp milk

Lay pastry on top and cut off edges. Mix together egg and milk and brush on top. Then cook in oven for about 45 minutes and serve either hot or cold.

'A true Aussie classic, this version comes from Lucinda McCook who was, for many years, in charge of the pastry section in various Hewitson restaurants.'

FURTHER THOUGHTS
on sausages

★ Bread patties are a great accompaniment (and one of the most popular recipes on 'Healthy, Wealthy & Wise'). Sauté $1/4$ chopped onion and 1 rasher of sliced bacon in a little oil. Then put 250 g of two-day-old toast bread into a bowl (crusts removed) with 1 cup milk. Mash with your hands and add to above, along with 2 eggs, 2 chopped spring (green) onions and seasonings. Then cook in pastry cutters or egg rings.

★ Make sausage patties by taking the skins off 'peasanty' Italian-style sausages and mixing the meat with sautéed chopped onion, fresh basil, garlic (if necessary) and a little sambal. Mix well, fry and serve between bread with roasted capsicum and a dollop of Dijon mustard mayo (see page 132).

★ Toad in the Hole is actually a rather whimsical name for sausages in Yorkshire pud. But it is tasty. Just combine 110 g plain flour and a good pinch of salt in a large bowl. Make a well in the centre and add 2 large eggs and 200 ml milk, little by little continually whisking. (Mixture should be reasonably thin.) Then put 3 tablespoons dripping or lard in an oven dish and, when smoking, pour a little batter in to cover bottom. Top with blanched, peeled sausages (see page 156), pour rest of batter over and around and cook at 220°C for 35—40 minutes.

★ Make sausage rolls by blanching and peeling sausages before wrapping in mustard-smeared puff pastry. Then brush with egg wash and bake until golden. Slice and serve with chutney, relish or tomato sauce.

Sausages with Brussels Sprout Colcannon Cakes

(SERVES 4)

olive oil	Heat a little oil in a large pan and gently
1 medium onion, chopped	sauté onion and bacon for a few minutes.
2 bacon rashers, sliced	Slice sprouts, toss in and gently cook for
6 brussels sprouts, any damaged leaves discarded	another 5 minutes.
4 large potatoes	Boil until tender then mash roughly with a fork.
1 egg	Add to potatoes, along with sprout mix and
2 tbsp chopped fresh parsley	mix well. Then, using a pastry cutter, form into patties.
4–8 thick sausages, blanched (see page 156)	Preheat and oil a grill. Cook sausages and colcannon cakes until bangers are golden brown and colcannon is crusty on the outer.
tomato chutney or mustard	Serve with chutney or mustard on the side.

'As I have mentioned before, brussels sprouts are one of those vegetables which you either love or hate. There seems to be no middle ground. I think it has a lot to do with the over cooking of same. (Over cooked brussels sprouts, in a similar vein to cabbage, release sulphur compounds which, while certainly not harmful to your health, are certainly off-putting to the appetite. But this is not the case when the sprouts are blanched until crisp-tender or briefly sautéed in hot oil or butter.)'

Cabbage, Cheese & Sausage Bake
(SERVES 6)

8 thick sausages, any variety

Preheat oven to 200°C.
Cook in simmering water until just firm when squeezed. Drain and, when cool enough to handle, remove skins.

$^1/_2$–1 savoy cabbage
table salt

Clean and remove core and any outer or damaged leaves. Shred, removing ribs, and then blanch in a large pot of lightly salted boiling water. Drain very well.

chicken stock, bought or homemade
  (see page 62)
grated tasty cheese

Put half of cabbage in a deep gratin dish. Cut sausages in thick slices and scatter over the top. Then top with rest of cabbage. Pour over a little stock and generously scatter with cheese and cook in oven for about 20 minutes until golden.

'A mound of creamy mashed spuds is a great accompaniment. Just cook 4–6 large potatoes until tender and then mash, adding up to $^3/_4$ cup of hot milk little by little. Season and finish with a good splash of cream and a dollop of butter.'

Black Pudding with Champ & Beetroot Chutney

(SERVES 4)

½ kg beetroot	Cook until tender. Then, when cool enough to handle, peel.
250 g onions	Coarsely chop onions and beetroot.
1 cup vinegar 1 cup sugar ½ tbsp rock salt ½ tbsp mustard seeds ½ tspn coriander seeds ½ tspn allspice berries, crushed freshly ground pepper	Put in a pot along with onion and beetroot and gently simmer for 30–40 minutes until thick. Cool.
Champ (see page 244)	Prepare and keep warm.
vegetable oil 16 thick slices black pudding	Heat a thin layer of oil in a large pan and fry black pudding in two lots until crispy on both sides. Drain well. Serve around the champ with a dollop of chutney.

'Black pudding, which we all either love or hate (I love it), is supposedly the most ancient of sausages, which even rated a mention in Homer's Odyssey, which appeared around 1000 BC.'

Spaghetti Puttanesca • Spaghetti Carbonara Penne Salad with Parmesan Dressing • Penne with Broccoli & Blue Mascarpone Cream • Fettuccine with Salami & Olives in a Tomato & Chilli Sauce • Spaghetti Aglio e Olio • Lamb & Macaroni Pastitsio • Beef & Italian Sausage Lasagne • Fettuccine with Charred Radicchio & Rocket Spaghetti with Meatballs • Baked Penne with Garlic, Zucchini & Eggplant • Hot & Sour Noodles • Hokkien Noodles with Wonga Bok & BBQ Pork • Chicken & Udon Noodles in a Green Tea Broth • Roast Duck Soup Noodles Crispy Noodle Cake with Shiitake Mushrooms & Bok Choy • Chicken Chow Mein

Perfect Pasta & Noodles

A recent food research study conducted by a leading Sydney newspaper revealed that our most popular meals included Spaghetti Bolognaise at number 1 and Lasagne at number 3 (steak was, interestingly, at number 2 and there was nary a mention of lamb, chicken, pork or fish).

Now, I must admit, I was a little surprised. Not just by the overwhelming popularity of pasta, but also by the high rating of steak, which has to me, seemingly faded in popularity in recent years. In fact, so much so that I queried the results and came away with a feeling that the survey was, in fact, just a quick whip around the office staff (and let's be fair – journalists, including many who become restaurant critics, are not renowned for their sophisticated taste). That aside, Perfect Pasta has certainly been one of our more popular sections and its ease of preparation has obviously made pasta a huge hit in the home kitchen.

And let us not forget noodles which are, these days, almost as popular and I suppose I shouldn't really be surprised because, if it's possible, they could be even easier to cook.

Spaghetti Puttanesca

(SERVES 4)

table salt	Cook pasta in plenty of lightly salted
400 g spaghetti	boiling water until al dente (firm to the
olive oil	tooth). Then drain and toss with a little oil.
6 tbsp olive oil	Heat oil in a pan and gently sauté.
2 garlic cloves, crushed	
1 chilli, sliced	
6 large ripe tomatoes, diced	Add to pan, toss well and then toss through
3 anchovies, finely chopped	pasta (adding a little more oil if necessary).
1 heaped tbsp drained capers	
6 pitted black olives, chopped	
12 fresh basil leaves, sliced	
1 tbsp grated fresh parmesan	
freshly grated parmesan	Serve with parmesan on the side.

'This is a dead easy method of cooking spaghetti. Put in a large pot of boiling, salted water for exactly 2 minutes. Then give it a good stir, turn the heat off, cover and leave for exactly 4 minutes. Drain and use. (For other pasta varieties the method is the same, but the time will vary.)'

Spaghetti Carbonara

(SERVES 4)

table salt
400 g spaghetti

Cook in plenty of lightly salted boiling water until al dente (firm to the tooth). Then drain.

olive oil
6 slices pancetta, chopped
1 tbsp chopped fresh parsley
$^1/_4$ cup cream
$^1/_4$ cup chicken stock, bought or homemade (see page62)
4 tbsp freshly grated parmesan

While pasta is cooking, heat a little oil in a pan and gently sauté pancetta. Add parsley, cream, stock and parmesan, and simmer for 5 minutes.

2 egg yolks
freshly ground salt & pepper

Toss pasta, sauce and yolks together and generously season with pepper and then salt to taste.

'Spaghetti Carbonara or the Chimney Sweep's Pasta, was so named because of the generous sprinkling of black pepper (carbon). But, obviously, its origins have been forgotten, because I have rarely seen this dish with more than the normal small grinding.'

Penne Salad with Parmesan Dressing

(SERVES 4)

table salt	Cook in plenty of lightly salted boiling
250–300 g penne	water until al dente (firm to the tooth).
olive oil	Drain and toss with a little oil.
4 baby carrots, peeled & sliced	Add to pasta and toss well.
1 celery stalk, sliced	
2–3 spring (green) onions, sliced	
3 ripe red tomatoes, cored & diced	
2 tbsp chopped fresh parsley	
2 tbsp chopped fresh basil	
juice of 1 lemon	Whisk together.
2 tbsp sherry vinegar	
2 tbsp grain mustard	
1 garlic clove, crushed	
$1/2$ cup olive oil	Add oil little by little. Then add parmesan,
$1/2$ cup freshly grated parmesan	sour cream and lemon juice and fold into
2 tbsp sour cream	pasta salad.
$1/2$ lemon	

'I have often had grumbles from viewers about the fact that their pasta sticks together when they cook it. I have always found that if you separate the pasta with a pair of tongs when you first put it in the boiling water, it will stay separate. (And, another thing, always add pasta to rapidly boiling water and cover the pot until it comes back to boil.)'

Penne with Broccoli & Blue Mascarpone Cream

(SERVES 4)

$^1/_4$ cup cream

1 cup vegetable stock, bought or homemade
(see page 198)

50 g soft blue cheese, crumbled

50 g mascarpone cheese

2 tbsp chopped fresh parsley

freshly ground pepper

Put in a pan and bring to the boil. Whisk well and then simmer to reduce, until thickish.

table salt

400 g penne

Cook in plenty of lightly salted boiling water, until al dente (firm to the tooth).

$^1/_2$ small head broccoli, cut into flowerets

When pasta is almost ready, add broccoli and bring back to the boil. Drain and toss well with cream mix.

'I first tasted this in Italy where it was made with Mascarpone Torta, which is sort of like a layered cake made from separate layers of mascarpone and gorgonzola. When making the sauce, the chef reduced pure cream and then scooped large spoonfuls of the torta into it. It was delicious, but I think it was about the richest dish I have ever tasted – so here I have cut it back with some vegie stock.'

Fettuccine with Salami & Olives in a Tomato & Chilli Sauce

(SERVES 4)

olive oil
1 onion, finely chopped
2 garlic cloves, finely sliced
2 chillies, finely sliced

Heat a little oil in a pot and gently sauté vegies for 2–3 minutes.

800 g canned diced tomatoes, drained a little
freshly ground salt & pepper
20 small black olives

Add and gently simmer for 10 minutes or so until thick and fragrant.

table salt
400 g fettuccine

At the same time, cook pasta in plenty of lightly salted boiling water until al dente (firm to the tooth).

6 slices hot salami, finely sliced
10 basil leaves, finely sliced

Add to sauce and cook for a few minutes.

freshly grated parmesan

Drain pasta and put in bowls. Then top with sauce and a sprinkling of cheese.

'Handwritten sign seen on the door of a Tuscan hotel's dining room (after many bad meals): 'Kindly to please not be complaining about the food. The chef is very nervous.' I think I would be nervous too – about eating there that is.'

FURTHER THOUGHTS
on the history of pasta

★ Although it is often thought that Marco Polo introduced pasta to Italy, having bought it home from China in 1298, there are many reports of pasta-like substances and machinery for centuries before that (including an estate list in Genoa dated 1279 which listed a 'bariscella piena de macaronis' (a basket full of macaroni). This may not predate Marco Polo by much, but pre-date it does.

★ Macaroni was then, in fact, a general description for pasta — not the tubular shape as we know it today. It wasn't until the Middle Ages that vermicelli (little worms) was introduced as the thin strands of current times.

★ During Mussolini's rise to power, it was rumoured that he proposed to ban the consumption of pasta because he considered it to be responsible for the low state of the Italian people (in a similar vein to a group called the futurists who denounced it as a symbol of oppressive dullness, plodding deliberation and fat bellied conceit).'

★ Pasta was first produced by mechanical means in Naples in 1878 (this caused a riot among the artisan pasta makers). In 1882 British-made kneaders, extruders and cutters were installed and in 1933 the firm of Braibanti unveiled the first completely mechanised continuous production line.

★ And a little bit of trivia. When Catherine de Medici married King Henri II in 1533, she took her cooks with her and the wedding banquet included one dish of pasta dressed with the juices of the roast (still a popular dish in Italy) and one sweet version with butter, sugar, cinnamon, honey and saffron.

Source: The Oxford Companion to Food

Spaghetti Aglio e Olio
(SERVES 4)

table salt 400 g spaghetti	Cook in plenty of lightly salted boiling water until al dente (firm to the tooth). Then drain.
8 tbsp olive oil 3 garlic cloves, finely chopped 2 chillies, finely sliced 2 anchovies, chopped	When pasta is ready, heat oil in a pan and gently sauté garlic and chilli. Then add anchovies and mix well.
2 tbsp chopped fresh parsley 3 tbsp freshly grated parmesan crusty bread	Toss pasta and sauce together. Serve with more parmesan on the side and plenty of crusty bread to soak up the juices.

'A recently published report by Professor Mark Wahlquist from Monash University in Melbourne states that capsaicin, the hot component in chillies, speeds up the body's metabolism so that eating chillies burns more calories quickly. (On that basis I should be about 3 stone.)'

Lamb & Macaroni Pastitsio

(SERVES 6–8)

olive oil
2 large onions, chopped
1 medium carrot, peeled & diced
2 celery stalks, diced
2 garlic cloves, crushed

Heat a little oil in a pot and gently sauté vegies until soft.

750 g minced lamb
800 g canned diced tomatoes, drained a little
1^1/$_2$ cups canned tomato puree
3 bay leaves
^{1}/$_2$ cup beef stock, bought or homemade
   (see page 128)
freshly ground salt & pepper

Add meat, stir and cook until it changes colour. Then add rest of ingredients and simmer until thick and fragrant (adding a little more stock if necessary).

table salt
400 g macaroni
olive oil

While meat sauce is cooking, cook pasta in plenty of lightly salted boiling water. Drain and toss with a little oil.

Mornay Sauce (see page 111)
grated tasty cheese
freshly grated parmesan

Preheat oven to 200°C.
Layer a lightly oiled baking dish with macaroni, parmesan, meat sauce and mornay (in that order). Then top with tasty cheese and cook in oven for about 30 minutes until golden and bubbling.

'The best way to check if pasta is ready is to simply try a piece (or pieces as the case may be – I begin trying dried pasta after about 6 minutes). It should be tender, yet still with a little resistance.'

Beef & Italian Sausage Lasagne

(SERVES 6–8)

olive oil
2–3 onions, chopped
2 garlic cloves, crushed

Preheat oven to 220°C.
Heat a little oil in a large pot and gently sauté vegies.

6 thick Italian sausages, peeled
600 g minced lean beef

Add and cook, stirring well to break up lumps, until colour has changed.

400 g canned diced tomatoes, drained a little
1 heaped tbsp tomato paste
$^3/_4$ cup tomato-based pasta sauce
$^3/_4$ cup red wine
$^1/_2$ tspn dried thyme
$^1/_2$ tspn dried oregano
1 tbsp chopped fresh rosemary needles
freshly ground salt & pepper

Add, mix well and simmer for about $^3/_4$ hour until thick and fragrant (adding a little more pasta sauce if necessary).

instant lasagne sheets
Mornay Sauce (see page 111)
grated tasty cheese
freshly grated parmesan

Spread a layer of meat sauce in a baking dish. Top with lasagne sheets, more meat sauce and then mornay. Repeat process, finishing with mornay. Then sprinkle with both cheeses and cook in oven for about 30 minutes until golden and bubbling.

'Of course you could use canned tomato puree instead of the pasta sauce, but I think the pasta sauce adds depth and a richness of flavour (particularly if it's the Iain Hewitson brand).'

Fettuccine with Charred Radicchio & Rocket

(SERVES 4)

table salt 400 g fettuccine	Cook in plenty of lightly salted boiling water until al dente (firm to the tooth). Then drain.
4 tbsp olive oil 1 red onion, finely sliced 1 garlic clove, finely sliced 1 chilli, finely sliced	At the same time, heat oil in a pan and gently sauté vegies, covered, over a low heat. Then toss with pasta in a large bowl.
1 head of radicchio, outer & damaged leaves removed & washed well olive oil spray	Also at the same time, cut radicchio in half, remove core and spray with oil. Cook on a ridged grill until lightly charred around the edges.
1 handful baby rocket freshly ground salt & pepper	Slice radicchio and add to pasta, along with rocket and seasonings.
freshly grated parmesan	Mound pasta in bowls and sprinkle with parmesan.

 'I have always thought that al dente meant 'firm to the bite'. But although the sentiment is correct, it actually means 'to the tooth'.'

Spaghetti with Meatballs

(SERVE 4–6)

olive oil
1 large onion, finely chopped
1 garlic clove, crushed

Heat a little oil in a pot and gently sauté vegies for a few minutes.

3–400 g lean beef mince
1 tspn sambal oelek
1 heaped tspn ground cumin
1 tbsp chopped fresh parsley
a splash of soy sauce
freshly ground salt & pepper

Put in a bowl, add half the onion mix and stir well.

800 g canned diced tomatoes, drained a little
1 tspn sambal oelek
1 tspn paprika
2 bay leaves
1 tspn caster sugar
$1/2$ cup chicken stock, bought or homemade
   (see page 62)
freshly ground salt & pepper

Add to pot with rest of the onion mix, and gently cook until thick (adding more stock if necessary). At the same time, form meat mix into meatballs and fry in a lightly oiled pan until sealed and crusty. Drain well and add to sauce.

table salt
400 g spaghetti
freshly grated parmesan

Cook pasta in plenty of lightly salted boiling water until al dente (firm to the tooth). Then drain, put in bowls and top with sauce and meatballs. Sprinkle with parmesan.

'Although the sauce was obviously derived from Italy, spaghetti with meatballs is actually an American creation (and just out of interest the United States, in particular North and South Dakota, is the world's largest producer of durum wheat, an essential ingredient in the production of good dried pasta).'

Hi
Hewy - Baby!

You must be sick of people especially the
ladies telling you how much they enjoy your
program, but we really do. Even my husband
who will be 89 this year watches every day,
but he's not so keen on the amount of garlic
you use. I've enclosed a recipe for apple
pudding which I thought might amuse you
as you seem to have a good sense of humour.
I came across it in a very old book that
belonged to my mother. I most probably ate
it when I was little girl – that was many years ago! By the way, my mother,
God bless her, was 94 when she died which was also a very long time ago!
Flo NSW

I have two complaints. I hope you don't mind, Iain. You once said, 'Never
scrape the garlic from the garlic press with the sharp blade of the knife', but as
my husband pointed out, you constantly do this. And another thing. I'll bet
your mother said to never have the handle of a pot or pan over the edge of the
stove or grill. Naughty Iain!
Jean QLD

My granddaughter is just three years of age and you are her favourite – forget
about the Wiggles, Humphrey etc. She watches you every day and calls me
when you cook. When the advertisements come on she tells my daughter (her
mother) to bring you back. If you are making your adult audience as happy as
my little Tahlia, well then, please keep it up.
Patricia VIC

Baked Penne with Garlic, Zucchini & Eggplant

(SERVES 4)

olive oil
1 large onion, chopped
1 garlic clove, crushed

Preheat oven to 200°C.
Heat a little oil in a pot and gently sauté until soft.

1–2 medium eggplants, cubed
3 medium zucchini, cubed

Throw in and toss for 1–2 minutes.

800 g canned diced tomatoes, drained
$^1/_2$ cup vegetable stock, bought or homemade
   (see page 198)
freshly ground salt & pepper

Add and gently cook until thick.

table salt
400 g penne
pesto, bought or homemade (see page 198)

At the same time, cook in lots of lightly salted boiling water until al dente (firm to the tooth). Then drain and toss into sauce with pesto to taste.

freshly grated parmesan

Put in an oven dish, sprinkle parmesan cheese over the top and bake for 20 minutes.

'This was one of the most requested pasta dishes. So, although it was featured in **The Huey Diet**, I felt it deserved another 15 minutes of fame.'

Hot & Sour Noodles

(SERVES 4–6)

3–4 Chinese sausages

Steam for 10 minutes. Then slice on the diagonal and set aside.

2 chillies, finely chopped
1 garlic clove, crushed
1 tspn freshly grated ginger
6 tbsp kecap manis
6 tbsp Chinese black vinegar
1 tbsp soy sauce
2 tbsp vegetable oil

Whisk together.

450 g Hokkien noodles
3 baby carrots, peeled & sliced on the diagonal
3 spring (green) onions, thickly sliced on the diagonal
12 snowpeas, halved crossways on the diagonal

Throw noodles into a large pot of boiling water. Stir to separate and then add vegies. Stir and strain well.

½ cup beanshoots
3 slices pickled ginger, sliced

Toss noodle mix in a bowl with beanshoots, ginger, Chinese sausage and dressing to taste. Serve in individual bowls.

'Forget Vegemite. I love this tart spicy dressing so much I reckon I could eat it on toast.'

Hokkien Noodles with Wonga Bok & BBQ Pork

(SERVES 4)

450 g Hokkien noodles	Soak in hot water for 10 minutes. Then drain and set aside.
vegetable oil	Heat a little oil in a wok and sauté for
2 tspn freshly grated ginger	1–2 minutes.
2 garlic cloves, crushed	
2 chillies, sliced	
1 tbsp soy sauce	Add and reduce a little.
4 tbsp chicken stock, bought or homemade (see page 62)	
1 tbsp Chinese wine	
a splash of oyster sauce	
$^1/_4$–$^1/_2$ tspn sesame oil	
$^1/_2$ wonga bok (Chinese white cabbage), cored & shredded	Add and cook for 1–2 minutes. Then add noodles and toss well, just to reheat.
200–300 g bought BBQ pork	
2 spring (green) onions, sliced	Serve in a bowl garnished with spring onion.

'It is always confusing buying Asian vegetables – particularly in different states. Wonga bok (which is also known as wong bak, wongah bak, Peking cabbage and even if my memory serves me correctly, napa cabbage) is the Chinese white cabbage with the slightly conical shape.'

Chicken & Udon Noodles in a Green Tea Broth

(SERVES 4)

200 g udon noodles	Cook as per below.
4 tspn green tea	Bring 3 cups of water to the boil. Leave for 2 minutes and then add tea. (Boiling water makes green tea bitter.)
2 skinless chicken breasts, sliced 2 tbsp soy sauce 1 tbsp kecap manis 1 tbsp mirin $^1/_2$ tbsp freshly grated ginger a splash of sesame oil	Toss together and leave for 30 minutes.
16 sugar peas, topped & tailed 4 baby carrots, peeled & sliced on the diagonal 4 water chestnuts, sliced	Bring tea to a simmer in pot and add chicken, marinade and vegies. Cook for 3 minutes, regularly stirring.
a splash of Chinese black vinegar 2 tbsp chopped fresh coriander soy sauce $^1/_2$ cup bean shoots	Add along with noodles, stir and serve in deep bowls.

 'Terry Durack in his book **Noodle** gives this method for cooking udon noodles (they can easily be over cooked and gluggy). Place noodles in a pot of boiling water. When the water comes back to the boil add 1 cup cold water. When it returns to the boil, add another cup of cold water. Repeat once or twice more until the noodles are soft, but not sloppy. Rinse under cold running water, drain well and set aside.'

Roast Duck Soup Noodles

(SERVES 4)

450 g Hokkien noodles

Soak in warm water for 10 minutes and then drain.

vegetable oil
2 garlic cloves, crushed
1 heaped tspn freshly grated ginger

Heat a little oil in a wok and quickly sauté.

1 tspn sambal oelek
2 cups chicken stock, bought or homemade
   (see page 62)
$^1/_4$ cup Japanese soy sauce
$^1/_4$ cup sake
$^1/_4$ cup mirin (Japanese rice wine)

Add, stir well and bring to the boil.

1 pkt baby corn
16 sugar peas
$^1/_2$ Chinese BBQ duck, cut the Chinese way

Add and simmer for a few minutes.

$^1/_4$ wonga bok (Chinese white cabbage), sliced
3 baby bok choy, separated into leaves

Add along with noodles and toss to wilt vegies. Then put in a large bowl (or bowls).

'You can serve this individually, but the Chinese would normally serve a soupish dish such as this as part of a number of dishes or, on special occasions, as part of a banquet.'

Crispy Noodle Cake with Shiitake Mushrooms & Bok Choy

(SERVES 2)

8 dried shiitake mushrooms	Soak in warm water for 15 minutes Then drain and slice (discarding stems).
1 x 200 g packet rice stick noodles sesame oil	Plunge noodles into a pot of boiling water for 1 minute. Then run under cold water, drain very well and toss with a little sesame oil.
vegetable oil	Heat 2 tbsp vegie oil in a non-stick omelette pan. Add noodles and press down to form a cake. Fry for about 5 minutes, adding a little more oil if necessary. When golden brown, turn out, re-oil pan and cook on the other side.
$^1/_4$ cup vegetable stock, bought or homemade (see page 198) 2 tbsp soy sauce 2 tbsp oyster sauce	Combine.
vegetable oil 1 garlic clove, finely chopped 1 tspn freshly grated ginger 4 heads baby bok choy, cleaned & halved length ways	When you turn the cake, heat a little oil in a wok, add garlic and ginger and toss for a few seconds. Then add shiitakes, bok choy and sauce and cook, stirring for a few minutes. To serve, put noodle cake on a plate and top with vegies and sauce.

'Any stirfry (meat or otherwise) works well with this crispy noodle cake.'

Chicken Chow Mein

(SERVES 4)

vegetable oil 1 garlic clove, crushed 1 tspn freshly grated ginger	Heat a little oil in a wok and sauté.
4 chicken thighs, boned & cubed	Add and toss well.
³/₄ cup chicken stock, bought or homemade (see page 62) 2 tbsp soy sauce 1 tbsp oyster sauce 2 tspn sesame oil	Add and gently simmer.
250 g chow mein noodles vegetable oil	At the same time, cover noodles with boiling water, leave for 5 minutes and drain. Then heat a little oil in a pan and fry noodles until they have some colour. Put in bowls.
1 cup shredded wonga bok (Chinese white cabbage) a good handful bean shoots 12 snowpeas, shredded 4 spring (green) onions, cut into 1 cm lengths	Add to chicken mix, toss well for 1 minute and then mound on top of noodles.

'My mate, Melbourne food writer Bob Hart, and I decided that it would be a bit of fun to visit our greatest Chinese restaurant, the Flower Drum, and order the old classics. Ruth and I joined him and his wife Iris and ate everything from spring rolls and chicken and sweetcorn soup to sweet and sour pork and chicken chow mein (and, of course, finished with banana fritters). I can't say it was a surprise because everything at the Flower Drum is brilliant, but some of these oldtime classics were really surprisingly good.'

Leek & Cheese Bread & Butter Pudding • Middle Eastern Chickpea & Vegie Stew • Red Onion & Cheese Tart

• Mushroom 'Steak' Sandwich • Spinach & Goat's Cheese Quesadillas • Sweet Potato, Corn & Fennel Stew

with Red Capsicum Rouille 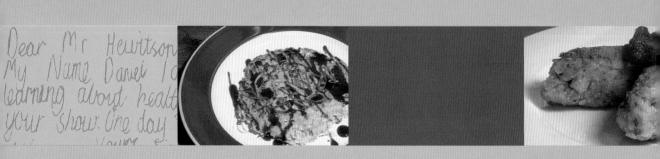 Mediterranean BBQ Sangas • Parmesan & Herb Crumbed Eggplant

with Pesto Mayonnaise • Lentil Burgers with Sweet & Sour Sauce Red Onion Tarte Tatin

with Goat's Cheese • Eggplant & Spinach Curry • Vegetarian 'Shepherd's' Pie • Vegetable Stock • Red

Cabbage Pancake with Asian Flavours • Carrot Osso Bucco • Glamorgan Sausages • Potato 'Pizza' with

Roasted Tomatoes, Fetta & Basil Oil Cheese Soufflé Pudding • Tomato, Cheese & Herb Clafoutis

Dear Mr Hewitson
My Name Daniel I
learning about healt
your show One day
Yours

Vegie Magic

In a similar vein to meat lovers (see page 103), not for one second would I ever suggest that vegetarians are pushier than the rest of us. But the second I meet a viewer who just happens to be a vego, I know that the first sentence will revolve around the fact that I don't cook enough vegetable-based dishes and, in fact, they haven't seen one on the show for months and months (or is that years and years).

Of course I forgive them, because I too am a great lover of vegies. But to prove them a little bit wrong, here are a small selection of some of our most popular vegetarian recipes – and I do mean a SMALL selection because I have tonnes and tonnes of the blessed things.

And just to ensure that vegos don't think that they are the only ones who complain about show content, just recently a real bloke came up to me asking, 'Why don't you cook more real food rather than that pinko, vegie crap?' (For the edification of our younger viewers, pinko was 50s slang for anyone supposedly with communist leanings).

Leek & Cheese Bread & Butter Pudding

(serves 4–6)

6–8 soft bread rolls
soft butter

Preheat oven to 200°C.
Thickly slice rolls and butter on one side.

olive oil
6 leeks, well washed & sliced

Heat a little oil in a pan and gently sauté leeks, covered, until soft.

2 cups grated tasty cheese
$1/4$ cup cream
4 large eggs
freshly ground salt & pepper

Whisk together and add leeks. Mix well and season.

extra grated tasty cheese
extra cream

Lay half of the bread, buttered side up, in a deep baking dish. Top with leek mix and then the rest of bread, buttered side up. Sprinkle with more cheese and a little cream and cook in oven for 15–20 minutes until golden.

'I sometimes add a couple of peeled, cored and diced Granny Smith apples to the leek mix (just toss through the leeks once cooked). It adds an interesting flavour to the dish, as well as a different texture.'

Middle Eastern Chickpea & Vegie Stew

(SERVES 4)

olive oil 2 onions, chopped 2 garlic cloves, crushed	Heat a little oil in a pot and gently sauté vegies.
2 medium zucchini, cubed 1 green capsicum, cored, seeded & cubed 1 red capsicum, cored, seeded & cubed 2 baby Japanese eggplant, cut in thickish slices	Add and toss well for a few minutes.
2 tspn ground cumin 2 tspn ground coriander 1 tspn turmeric	Add and toss for 1 minute.
800 g canned diced tomatoes, drained a little 1 cup vegetable stock, bought or homemade (see page 198) freshly ground salt & pepper 1 tbsp harissa, bought or homemade (see below)	Add, mix well and gently cook for about 15 minutes until sauce is thick and fragrant (adding more stock if necessary).
1 cup canned chickpeas, rinsed well & drained chopped coriander yoghurt	Add chickpeas and coriander. Mix in well and check seasoning. To serve, put in bowls with a dollop of yoghurt on top.

'Harissa, a Middle Eastern chilli paste can be bought in many good delis. But if you want to make your own, just roast 2 tablespoons coriander seeds and 1 tablespoon cumin seeds in a hot, dry pan for a few minutes over a moderate heat. Then whiz up with 3 tablespoons olive oil, 4 fresh chillies, 2 garlic cloves and a pinch of salt. (It will keep for a month in the refrigerator.)'

Red Onion & Cheese Tart

(SERVES 1–2)

olive oil
3 large red onions, cut into wedges
freshly ground salt & pepper

Preheat oven to 180°C.
Heat a little oil in a non-stick pan, add onions, season and cover. Gently cook for about 10 minutes until tender. Then drain in a colander or sieve.

olive oil spray
1 bought pastry sheet
grated tasty cheese

Spray a baking sheet with a little oil. Put pastry on and top with onion and then cheese, leaving $1\frac{1}{2}$ cm border.

1 egg
2 tbsp milk

Beat together and brush around border. Cook in oven for 12–14 minutes until golden and bubbling.

'Bought pastry sheets are an asset in any kitchen, because at the drop of a hat you can throw together a simple yet delicious tart like this (or even a 'pizza' with the help of the kids).'

Mushroom 'Steak' Sandwich

(SERVES 4)

1 French bread stick
100 g soft butter
2 garlic cloves, crushed
juice of $\frac{1}{2}$ lemon
1 tbsp chopped fresh parsley

Preheat oven to 220°C.
Cut bread in half lengthways. Mix together butter, garlic, lemon and parsley and generously smear on both inner surfaces. Press back together and cook in oven until hot and crusty.

6 large flat field mushrooms, peeled & stalks discarded
freshly ground salt & pepper

At the same time, put in a baking tray and dot with leftover garlic butter. Season and cook on the upper shelf of oven until they have collapsed a bit and are very juicy.

pesto, bought or homemade (see page 42)
cos or iceberg lettuce leaves

Smear bottom half of bread with pesto, top with lettuce and mushrooms and press top firmly on. Then cut in 4 crossways.

'When I was young, I remember the family's mushroom foraging expeditions – nothing fancy just big, juicy field mushrooms which my mother simply cut in four and sautéed in lots of butter with chopped parsley and a good squeeze of lemon juice.'

Spinach & Goat's Cheese Quesadillas

(SERVES 4)

vegetable oil
1 garlic clove, crushed
$1/2$ onion, finely chopped
2 chillies, finely chopped

Heat a little oil in a pan and gently sauté vegies until softish.

500 g baby spinach leaves
freshly ground salt & pepper

At the same time, blanch spinach in plenty of lightly salted boiling water for 1 minute. Then drain very well and coarsely chop. Add to pan, toss well and season.

250 g soft goat's cheese
2 tbsp sour cream

Mix together.

8 large flour tortillas
grated tasty cheese

Lay 4 on a bench and smear with goats cheese (not quite to the edge), and top with spinach mix and grated tasty (don't overfill). Paint edge with water and press other tortillas on top.

vegetable oil

In a non-stick pan large enough to hold one quesadilla, heat a little oil and slide in. Cook over a moderate heat for about 2 minutes on each side, adding more oil as necessary.

roasted red capsicum rouille (see below)

Cut into wedges and sprinkle with rouille.

'You could serve these, as is traditional, with a simple tomato salsa, but I prefer roasted capsicum rouille made by whizzing up roasted red capsicum (see page 142) with mayonnaise, sour cream, 1–2 garlic cloves and a squeeze of fresh lemon juice.'

Sweet Potato, Corn & Fennel Stew with Red Capsicum Rouille

(SERVES 4–6)

olive oil

1 large onion, chopped

1–2 fennel bulbs, cored & finely sliced

2 garlic cloves, crushed

Heat a little oil in a large heavy-bottomed pot and gently sauté vegies until soft.

2 medium sweet potatoes, peeled & cubed

3 corn cobs, kernels removed

800–1200 g canned diced tomatoes, drained

1½ cups vegetable stock, bought or
   homemade (see page 198)

a pinch of saffron threads

1 heaped tspn fresh thyme leaves

freshly ground salt & pepper

2 bay leaves

Add, stir well and gently simmer for about 15 minutes until thick and fragrant.

red capsicum rouille (see page 189)

Mound into bowls and sprinkle with rouille.

 'I am often asked why, in this modern age, I continue to advocate using wooden spoons when cooking stews, braises, etc. Apart from the fact that, to me, the scrape of a stainless steel spoon on a pot is akin to the scraping of chalk on the blackboard, wooden spoons are relatively heatproof, won't have an adverse effect on acidic food, don't scratch non-stick surfaces and, getting right down to the nitty gritty, feel comfortable in the hand.'

Dear Huey...

>I really enjoy watching your show, but your pronunciation of piquancy is a constant annoyance. I have even heard another TV cook using it (possibly due to your influence). My husband and I have worked for many years with the various editors of the Macquarie Dictionary. We can't believe we would have been the first to point out that 'piquant' is pronounced with a 'k', not like the sound in 'queen', but like the sound in 'cat'. As this is indeed one of your favourite words, please get it right!
Kim & Michael

>I just love your show. I've had such a disastrous year through no fault of my own, but I turn on at 11 am Perth time and have such a giggle at your antics, i.e. cooking for 20,000 or dropping potatoes on the floor. You are a legend and make me happy for 30 minutes, good onya love. Keep up the excellent humour.
Giuly WA

>I recently blew out to 355 kg. Over the past eight months I have lost 70 kg. Although I have always dieted, you have encouraged me to try new things but to remain healthy rather than the old lean chicken and boring salad. I just wanted you to know you that you helped me.
Big Jim

>You so sexy (kiss)
Anna

Mediterranean BBQ Sangas

(SERVES 4)

$^1/_2$ cup olive oil
2 garlic cloves, crushed
freshly ground salt & pepper

Preheat BBQ or ridged grill.
Whisk together.

1 medium eggplant, sliced
2 medium zucchini, sliced

Oil the grill and cook, regularly brushing
with garlic oil.

1 French bread stick, cut in 4 crossways
6 semi-dried tomatoes, sliced
3 ripe red tomatoes, sliced
6 bocconcini, sliced
2 roasted red capsicum (see page 142)
12 pitted black olives, sliced
10 basil leaves, sliced

Cut bread pieces in half horizontally,
hollow bottom out a little and brush with
garlic oil. Then layer with both tomatoes,
bocconcini, capsicum, olives, basil and BBQ
vegies. Press top on firmly, wrap in foil and
put on barbie or grill for 5–6 minutes,
turning once or twice. Slice and serve.

'I will definitely get shot down for mentioning this in the vegetarian section
but you can, if you like, add meats such as salami or prosciutto, a variety of
cheeses and, if you have a truly sophisticated palate – anchovies.'

Parmesan & Herb Crumbed Eggplant with Pesto Mayonnaise

(SERVES 4)

2–3 medium eggplant	Cut into $^3/_4$ cm thick rounds.
1 cup breadcrumbs 1 heaped tbsp freshly grated parmesan 1 tbsp chopped fresh parsley	Mix together and put in a bowl.
plain flour 2 eggs 1 cup milk	Put flour in another bowl and whisk eggs and milk in a third. Then dust eggplant with flour, dip into egg wash and firmly press into crumbs.
olive oil	Heat a layer of oil in a large non-stick pan and fry the eggplant in 3 or 4 lots until golden (don't overcrowd pan). Drain well on paper towels.

$^3/_4$ cup mayonnaise, bought or homemade
  (see page 23)
2 tbsp sour cream
1 heaped tbsp pesto, bought or homemade
  (see page 42)
	Mix together and serve on the side.

'At the risk of sounding completely mad, female eggplant supposedly have less seeds than their male counterparts (you can tell a female by its slight indentation). But whatever the sex, make sure you buy eggplant that are smooth, very shiny and heavy for their size.'

Lentil Burgers with Sweet & Sour Sauce

(SERVES 4)

3 tbsp vegetable oil
2 large onions, finely chopped
1 medium carrot, finely diced
1 celery, stalk finely diced

Put in a pan, cover and gently cook for 20 minutes.

1 cup red lentils

At the same time, place in a pot, add water to cover and cook for 20–30 minutes, until just tender. Drain well and crush a little in a blender or processor.

2 tbsp chopped fresh herbs
1 egg
1 cup breadcrumbs
freshly ground salt & pepper

Mix lentils, vegies, herbs, egg, crumbs and seasonings Then spread out on a tray and leave to cool.

200 ml pineapple juice
1 tbsp rice vinegar
1 tbsp Chinese wine or dry sherry
2 tbsp soy sauce
2 tbsp caster sugar
3 tbsp tomato sauce
1 tbsp cornflour

While cooling, put everything except cornflour in a pot and boil for 1 minute. Then mix cornflour and 1 tablespoon water together and whisk in. Keep warm.

breadcrumbs
vegetable oil
1 continental (telegraph) cucumber, sliced
   on the diagonal

Form lentil mix into burgers and lightly crumb. Then heat a thin layer of oil in a large non-stick pan and fry on both sides until golden. Put cucumber on plates, top with burgers and drizzle sauce over the top (serve extra on the side).

'As a vegetarian, you have to remember the phrase 'a balanced diet' – and pulses such as lentils play a very important role in such a diet.'

Red Onion Tarte Tatin with Goat's Cheese

(SERVES 2)

4 medium red onions	Preheat oven to 200°C. Halve and slice, keeping root end intact. Then put in an omelette pan, round side down.
caster sugar red wine balsamic vinegar freshly ground salt & pepper soft butter	Sprinkle with sugar, wine and balsamic. Season well and dot with butter. Then cook in oven for 30 minutes, adding more liquid if drying out (the finished juices should be lightly caramelised not liquid).
a sheet of puff pastry 1 egg 3 tbsp milk	Cut pastry to cover the pan and place on top, folding edges in a bit. Then mix egg and milk together and brush the top. Cook in oven until golden, then place a plate on top and turn out.
2–4 thin slices soft goat's cheese baby rocket, dressed with a little olive oil	Heat overhead grill. Place goat's cheese on onion and grill until melted. Top with baby rocket.

'Traditionally, tarte tatin is an upside down French tart which is made with apples and named after the Tatin sisters who created it in their restaurant in Lamotte – Beavron. But these days, tarte tatins are created using many different ingredients. (I recently tasted a mango one in a restaurant which shall remain nameless – it was bloody awful.)'

Eggplant & Spinach Curry

(SERVES 4)

2 cups vegetable oil
6 Japanese eggplant, sliced & quartered

In a wok, heat oil to smoking and fry eggplant in 3 or 4 lots until golden. Drain well on paper towels. Then strain oil and set aside for other uses.

a little of the above oil
1 heaped tspn freshly grated ginger
1 large onion, finely chopped
2 chillies, sliced
2 garlic cloves, crushed

Throw the oil back into wok and sauté vegies until golden.

4 cardamom pods, lightly crushed
1 tspn garam masala
$^1/_2$ tspn ground turmeric
$^1/_2$ tspn ground cumin
2 cloves

Add and toss to release aromas.

1 cup coconut cream
200 g canned diced tomatoes, drained a little
$^1/_2$ cup vegetable stock
1 cinnamon stick
1 tbsp Dijon mustard

Add half the coconut cream along with the rest of the ingredients. Simmer until a sauce-like consistency, adding rest of coconut cream as you do so.

a large handful of baby spinach, well washed
Rice Pilaf (see page 105)

Toss in, along with eggplant, and cook for about 2 minutes. Serve on rice pilaf.

'A mild yet flavoursome curry, I often serve this as an entree or starter particularly when the main course is something a little plain.'

Vegetarian 'Shepherd's' Pie

(SERVES 4–6)

olive oil

1 large red capsicum, cored, seeded & diced

1 large onion, chopped

2 celery stalks, diced

2 small leeks, well washed & sliced

2 medium carrots, peeled & diced

1 garlic clove, crushed

Heat a little oil in a large pot and gently sauté vegies until softish.

800 g canned diced tomatoes, drained a little

$1/4$ cup tomato based pasta sauce

1 cup vegetable stock, bought or homemade
(see page 198)

$1/4$ cup dry white wine

2 bay leaves

freshly ground salt & pepper

Add, mix well and gently cook until thick.

2–3 sweet potatoes, peeled & cut in chunks

a good dollop of butter

freshly ground salt & pepper

At the same time, cook sweet potatoes until tender. Then drain and mash with butter and seasonings. Keep warm.

400 g canned cannelini beans, drained
& rinsed

2 tbsp chopped fresh basil

Preheat oven to 220°C.
When stew is cooked, add beans and basil. Mix well and check seasoning.

grated tasty cheese

Put stew in an oven dish, top with sweet potato and a generous amount of cheese. Then cook in oven for about 15 minutes until golden brown.

'You could, of course, leave the cheese off (and, if you must, leave the butter out of the sweet potato mash too).'

Vegetable Stock

(FOR APPROX 2–3 LITRES)

2 leeks, washed & coarsely chopped
2 onions coarsely chopped
6 tomatoes, washed & coarsely chopped
4 celery stalks, washed & coarsely chopped
4 garlic cloves, washed & coarsely chopped
60 g soft herbs
2 lemons, sliced
4 litres cold water
2 star anise
2 good slurps white wine
freshly ground salt & pepper

Put in a large pot and rapidly boil for 20 minutes. Cool, then strain through muslin and refrigerate.

'When making stocks, do not peel the vegies.'

Red Cabbage Pancake with Asian Flavours

(SERVES 4)

1 cup plain flour, sifted 1 egg a good splash of soy sauce a good pinch of sugar $^1/_2$ cup vegetable stock, bought or homemade 　　(see page 198) freshly ground salt & pepper	Combine in a bowl.
150 g red cabbage, finely sliced & ribs 　　removed 1 medium carrot, peeled & grated 1 heaped tbsp pickled ginger, finely sliced 1 spring (green) onion, finely sliced	Add and mix well.
vegetable oil	Heat a little oil in a non-stick omelette pan and spoon in a thinnish layer of batter. Cook until golden on both sides. Then remove, keep warm and continue until all batter is used.
kecap manis 1–2 spring (green) onions, finely sliced on 　　the diagonal	Sprinkle with kecap manis and spring onion.

'In my files, it doesn't say where this dish comes from but it's a ripper and I've even been known to reheat leftovers in the microwave for brekkie (on the rare occasion that there are leftovers).'

Carrot Osso Bucco

(SERVES 4)

2 tbsp olive oil

6 medium carrots, peeled & thickly sliced on the diagonal

Heat oil in a pot and cook carrots for about 5 minutes until lightly browned.

1 medium onion, chopped

1 celery stalk, diced

1 garlic clove, crushed

800 g canned diced tomatoes, drained a little

$^1/_2$ cup vegetable stock, bought or homemade (see page 198)

2 bay leaves

1 tspn fresh thyme leaves

1 tbsp chopped fresh parsley

1 thick slice of orange

Add, turning heat down and cooking very gently for 7–8 minutes, adding more stock if necessary. When carrots are glazed and tender, put in a bowl.

Lemon Rice (see page 233)

Serve with rice.

'On our last visit to Paris, Ruth and I were lucky enough to snare a table at Le Grand Vefour. It was one of the best meals I have had in a French restaurant (it got three stars in Michelin soon after). What set it apart was chef Guy Martin's use of basic ingredients. I had braised oxtail with garlic and olive mash, which, while sounding pretty ordinary, had the most amazing depth of flavour. In the same vein is his Carrot Osso Bucco, which I also think is a wonderful use of a rather basic ingredient.'

Glamorgan Sausages

(SERVES 4)

1–2 leeks, well washed, sliced & sautéed in oil until soft 150 g fresh breadcrumbs made from day-old bread 1 medium onion, finely chopped 2 eggs 1 cup grated tasty cheese 1 tbsp chopped fresh parsley a splash of green Tabasco freshly ground salt 1 heaped tspn Dijon mustard	In a large bowl, thoroughly mix together.
$^1/_4$ cup freshly grated parmesan $^1/_2$ cup bought breadcrumbs	Using your hands, form soft mixture into 'sausages'. Then combine parmesan and crumbs and carefully coat sausages.
vegetable oil	Shallow fry in moderately hot oil until golden on all sides. Drain well.
fresh tomato sauce (see page 219 or 233) or any relish or chutney	Serve on the side.

 'I am not terribly keen on the idea of making vegetarian dishes look like their meaty equivalents, e.g. nut cutlets, mock steak, etc. But with these sausages, I will make an exception (and they don't really look much like any bangers that I know).'

Potato 'Pizza' with Roasted Tomatoes, Fetta & Basil Oil

(SERVES 4)

table salt 6 large potatoes, washed	Cook in plenty of lightly salted boiling water for 10 minutes. Drain and cool (overnight would be good).
2 spring (green) onions, chopped 2 eggs freshly ground salt & pepper	Then peel and coarsely grate potatoes. Put in a bowl and mix in spring onions, eggs and seasonings. Set aside until ready to cook.
8–12 medium tomatoes, cored freshly ground salt & pepper olive oil	Preheat oven to 180°C. Put in a baking tray, season and sprinkle with oil. Cook in oven for about 30 minutes until they begin to collapse.
olive oil butter	At the same time, heat a little oil and butter in a small omelette pan and press a thinnish layer of potato into it. Cook until golden, then turn over and cook (adding more oil if necessary). Place in oven to keep hot and repeat process.
crumbled fetta cheese Basil Oil (see page 225)	When pizzas and tomatoes are ready, place potato 'pizza' on plates, top with tomatoes and sprinkle with fetta and basil oil.

'Instead of the basil oil you could smear the pizza with pesto, bought or homemade (see page 42) or olive paste before topping with the tomatoes and fetta.'

Hi
Hewy – Baby!

You are the best cook on TV, not only for your
culinary skills but your cheeky personality is
unique. I have an idea that could be
incorporated into your range of cookbooks.
My suggested title is 'Tasty Treats for
Toothless Tigers'. Australia's ageing
population is large and growing rapidly. It
needs a book with some of your lovely stews
and casseroles and the gumbo of course. But
Huey, go lightly on the chilli and capsicum
because of the reflux syndrome. How about it?
We oldies don't need to waste our time on chewing.
Beverley NSW

Whilst I enjoy your pragmatic approach to cooking, your presentation
absolutely appals me. A potentially delightful meal is reconstituted as an
unsteadily towering inferno with an excellent chance of causing
embarrassment to diners. The now imponderable heap then sits tenuously on a
huge plate. Aesthetically, dearie, it plain doesn't work! Please consider possible
logistics of some situations: unsteady hands, children, false teeth, geriatrics,
outdoor eating, finger food and so forth. We don't need skyscrapers.
Carol NSW

I would like to share this with your viewers. I cut herbs and spices, put them
into portions and freeze them. It's very handy when one is in a hurry and the
kitchen stays clean.
Ursula NSW

Cheese Soufflé Pudding

(SERVES 4)

2 tbsp butter 3 tbsp plain flour	Preheat oven to 190°C. Melt butter, add flour and gently cook.
1¼ cups milk	Heat milk and add to flour mixture, all at once. Whisk vigorously and gently cook for 5 minutes.
150 g grated gruyère cheese freshly ground salt & pepper a pinch of nutmeg	Add, mix in and remove from heat. Allow to cool a little.
3 large eggs, beaten 3 tbsp chopped fresh parsley ½ tbsp Dijon mustard butter	Thoroughly mix in eggs, parsley and mustard. Then pour into a lightly greased gratin dish and cook in oven for about 30 minutes until puffed and golden. Serve immediately.

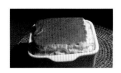

'A terrific light dish from American TV Chef and author Jacques Pepin.'

Tomato, Cheese & Herb Clafoutis

(SERVES 4)

6 ripe red tomatoes, cored & peeled
table salt

Preheat oven to 190°C.
To peel tomatoes, cut out core, put in a large pot of boiling water and count to ten. Then remove and plunge into cold water. The skins will slip off easily.
Slice tomatoes in 4 lengthways and place in one layer on paper towels. Generously salt and top with more towels. Leave for 20 minutes to mop up excess liquid and then put, in one layer, in a baking dish.

3 eggs
5 tbsp cream
2 tbsp snipped fresh chives
$^{1}/_{4}$ cup grated tasty cheese
freshly ground pepper

Whisk and pour over the top.

extra grated tasty cheese

Top with a little more cheese and cook in oven until puffed and golden (12–14 minutes). Serve immediately.

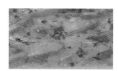 'Clafoutis is traditionally a baked custard or flan studded with cherries. And purists who bicker about whether the cherries should be pitted or not may be a little upset by this tomato version – but, who cares, it tastes good.'

Country Bread with Peppered Pears & Blue Cheese • Tunisian Chakchouka Pie Floater

Parsee Scrambled Eggs Oven Omelette with Baby Potatoes • Microwave Risotto with Roasted

Tomatoes & Crispy Pancetta • Stuffed Croissants • Cheese Fingers with Homemade Tomato Sauce • Fried

Egg Sandwich • Super-Dooper Hot Chocolate • Microwave Tomato Sauce • Cinnamon-Thyme Tea •

Moroccan Mint Tea • Chilli Infused Oil • Basil Infused Oil • Preserved Lemons

Dear Mr He
M name is Du
We have been
shows. Would
come to our s

Odds & Sods

This section is full of all those popular dishes which are hard to categorise. Snacks, brekkies, basics, quirky little numbers and anything else that doesn't quite fit into any section that I can think of. But, these have also been some of our most requested, purely and simply because they have also been, in most cases, amongst our easiest recipes – more destined to add a little something to a meal rather than play the starring role.

Country Bread with Peppered Pears & Blue Cheese

(SERVES 4)

2–3 firm pears, peeled & cored
olive oil
freshly ground pepper

Preheat both ridged and overhead grills.
Cut pears in 4 and toss with a little oil and
pepper. Then grill until slightly charred.

4 thick slices country-style bread

Brush with oil and grill on both sides.

thin slices of a softish blue cheese
baby rocket leaves

Place cheese on bread and put under
overhead grill until it just melts. Then
top with pears and rocket.

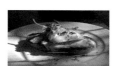

'A soft blue such as gorganzola or, closer to home, Milawa
Blue would work well in this dish. I often serve this as a
cheese course but have also, once or twice, served it as a
light supper (in which case I double the quantities).'

Tunisian Chakchouka

(SERVES 2)

olive oil
2 garlic cloves, sliced
1 small onion, finely sliced
1 chilli, sliced

Heat a little oil in a pan and gently sauté vegies.

1 red capsicum, cored, seeded & finely sliced
1 green capsicum, cored, seeded & finely sliced
6 button mushrooms, sliced
freshly ground salt & pepper

Add and cook for 5 minutes.

800 g canned diced tomatoes, drained
$1/4$ cup vegetable stock, bought or homemade (see page 198)
2 tbsp chopped fresh parsley

Add and cook until thick. Then spread out into an even layer across surface of pan.

2 large eggs
chopped fresh parsley

Make two separate indentations in the sauce with the back of a kitchen spoon and break in the eggs. Cover and cook until just set and garnish with parsley.

'A terrific brunch or light supper dish (where I serve it with a pile of lightly cooked, crispy green beans).'

Pie Floater

(SERVES 4)

2 large potatoes, peeled & chopped
3 large onions, peeled & chopped
chicken stock, bought or homemade
  (see page 62)
freshly ground salt & pepper

Preheat oven to 180°.
Put vegies in a pot, cover well with stock
and cook until tender.

3 cups frozen peas, thawed

Add and, the second the liquid comes back
to the boil, blend. Check seasoning.

4 meat party pies

At the same time, heat pies for about
8 minutes in oven.

bought tomato sauce (preferably in a
  squeezy bottle)

Put soup in flat bowls, top with a pie and
sprinkle sauce over the top.

'My "posh" version of that rather strange South Australian speciality which is served at pie carts throughout the state. And just to show that New Zealanders are strange too, we had our own unusual favourite – Pea, Pie and Pud which, as the name suggests, was a meat pie with mashed potatoes, peas and gravy, all piled on the top.'

Parsee Scrambled Eggs

(SERVES 2)

1 tbsp vegetable oil 1 tbsp butter $^1/_2$ onion, chopped 1 chilli, finely sliced	Heat oil and butter in a pan and gently sauté onion and chilli until soft.
a good pinch ground cumin a good pinch turmeric $^1/_2$ tbsp freshly grated ginger	Add and cook for 1 minute.
6 eggs a little cream freshly ground salt 1 large ripe tomato, cored & diced	Whisk together and add to pan. Gently scramble until soft curds form, stirring continually with a wooden spoon.
1 tbsp chopped fresh coriander toasted sourdough or pappadums	Mix in coriander and serve either with toasted sourdough or pappadums.

 'The Parsees of Western India are descendants of migrants from Afghanistan and Iran (in the 7th Century). The spicing of their food is moderate, few foods are prohibited and egg dishes are very popular.'

Oven Omelette with Baby Potatoes

(SERVES 4)

melted butter

Preheat oven to 200°C.
Generously brush a gratin dish with butter.

6 baby potatoes, well scrubbed & cooked until
   just tender
3 spring (green) onions, chopped
grated tasty cheese

Cut spuds into chunks and put in dish
along with spring onions and a small
handful of cheese.

6 eggs
2 tbsp cream
a splash of Tabasco
freshly ground salt
2 tbsp chopped fresh basil

Beat together, pour over the top and cook
in oven for about 15 minutes until puffed
and golden. Serve with a green salad.

'Always store potatoes in a cool, dark spot (not in the fridge) and always take them out of the plastic bag. And, keep in mind, the green on potatoes is caused by them being exposed to excessive light. The excess solanine which this causes can be poisonous, as are the leaves and fruit of the potato plant itself.'

Microwave Risotto with
Roasted Tomatoes & Crispy Pancetta

(SERVES 4)

4 medium tomatoes, cored & halved olive oil freshly ground salt & pepper	Preheat oven to 170°C. Season, drizzle with oil and cook in oven until they begin to collapse.
2 tbsp butter 2 tbsp olive oil	Cook in microwave for 2 minutes.
1 medium onion, finely chopped	Add, mix well and cook for 4 minutes.
1 cup arborio rice	Add, stir well and cook, uncovered, for another 4 minutes.
3 cups vegetable stock, bought or homemade (see page 198)	Add and cook, uncovered, for 9 minutes. Stir well and cook for another 9 minutes. Then sit for 5 minutes to absorb liquid.
$1/4$ cup freshly grated parmesan 1 tbsp chopped fresh parsley freshly ground salt & pepper	Mix in.
olive oil 8 slices pancetta, optional	When ready, heat a little oil in a pan and fry pancetta until crispy. Drain well on paper towels. Mound risotto in bowls, top with tomatoes, pancetta and extra parmesan, if you like.

'A cheat's risotto which is almost as good as the real, and very time consuming, thing.'

Dear Huey...

>I truly believe you are god
sent back to earth in human
form. your show is an inspiration
to us all and I cannot miss an
episode. Please make me a steak
on your show so I can marvel at
your brilliance.
Your biggest fan, Seven
PS I named my dog after you.

>I live in the Old Timers
Retirement Village where Big Huey
is required viewing. I conducted
a survey the other day, and the
cooking shows rated as follows:
Number 1: Big Huey
Number 2: Jamie Oliver
Number 3: Consuming Passions
Nigella didn't rate a place.
Doug NT

>I like the way you always let us in on little bits of
information and tips that make things better. My mother
and mother-in-law thinks it's just great that every
time I go to visit them I have a Huey tip for them.
Jo-Anne

>My 22 month old son gets so excited when your show
starts. He says your name constantly and giggles.
Thank you for making him happy.
Jenny

>Can you please not tell any of your jokes on air
because they don't have anything to do with cooking
and you make people lose interest in what you're doing.
Also, can you please cook a triple decker chocolate
cake with a lot of cream and strawberries in between
each layer and more on the top of the cake.
Big Boy Chubb Chubb

Stuffed Croissants

(SERVES 2–4)

4 croissants, sliced in half
3–4 pears, peeled, cored & sliced
8–12 slices ripe brie

Preheat oven to 200°C.
Place bottom halves on a baking sheet and top with pears and brie. Put tops on and bake in oven for 5–10 minutes until cheese is melted and croissants are hot.

a small handful of baby rocket
extra virgin olive oil
balsamic vinegar

In a bowl, toss rocket with oil and a little balsamic.
Place croissants on plates, remove lids, mound with rocket and then return lids.

'In New Zealand, there are a couple of country cafés called Brown Sugar (in Otaki and Taihape, if I remember correctly) which serve food like all country cafés should – simple, tasty and with lots of good old fashioned flair. This is my variation on one of their popular dishes. (They also stuff their freshly baked croissants with creamy scrambled eggs – delicious.)'

Cheese Fingers with Homemade Tomato Sauce

(SERVES 6–8)

1 kg ripe tomatoes, cored & chopped

250 g Granny Smith apples, peeled, cored & diced

150 g onions, chopped

$^5/_8$ cup white vinegar

200 g sugar

$^1/_2$ tspn allspice

1 tspn ground cloves

1 heaped tspn sambal oelek

1 tspn table salt

Put in a large pot, mix well and bring to the boil. Simmer for about $1^1/_4$ hours, regularly stirring. Blend and cool (if keeping, pour into sterilised jars).

---

500 g Colby cheese

Cut into thickish fingers.

---

plain flour

freshly ground salt & pepper

breadcrumbs

2 eggs

$^1/_2$ cup milk

Line up three bowls. Put flour, pepper and salt in one, eggs beaten with milk in another, and breadcrumbs in the third. Dust cheese fingers in flour then dip into egg wash and firmly press into crumbs.

---

6 cups vegetable oil

Heat oil to 180°–190°C in a pan (see page 15) and fry cheese fingers until golden (don't overcrowd the pan). Drain well on paper towels and serve with sauce on the side.

'This is my mother's famous tomato sauce, which you obviously make in a larger quantity than is necessary for this recipe purely and simply because it is delicious on almost anything.'

Fried Egg Sandwich

(SERVES 4)

4 thick slices country-style bread	Cut holes in the middle of bread with a pastry cutter.
vegetable oil a knob of butter	Put a thin layer of oil in a large non-stick pan, add butter and cook bread on one side until golden.
4 large eggs freshly ground salt & pepper	Turn, break an egg into each hole, season and gently cook until egg is just set.
tomato ketchup, optional	Serve with a good dollop of ketchup (and bacon, sausages, etc. if you like).

'If you are a bit of a male romantic, for your wife or girlfriend's birthday (or on Valentine's Day), instead of using a round pastry cutter, use a heart-shaped one – I promise you will win lots of brownie points.'

Super-Dooper Hot Chocolate

(SERVES 1)

1 large mug of milk
1 tspn sugar
a few drops of vanilla extract

Gently heat in a small pot.

50 g dark cooking chocolate

When almost boiling, add and stir until melted.

whipped cream
grated chocolate

Pour into a mug and top with cream and chocolate.

'Hot chocolate is an ancient drink. The Maya from the 1st millennium drank it with chillies and vanilla, the Aztecs preferred to add the seeds and petals of various herbs and flowers, while the Spaniards introduced the practice of adding cane sugar. (I must admit that, although I am a lover of chillies, I can't quite get my head around the idea of adding the odd chilli to my hot chockie).'

Microwave Tomato Sauce

(MAKES 500 ML)

6 ripe tomatoes, cored & coarsely chopped

½ red onion, coarsely chopped

½ red capsicum, cored, seeded & coarsely chopped

1 tbsp chopped fresh parsley

3 tbsp olive oil

1 tspn sambal oelek

1 tspn soy sauce

freshly ground salt & pepper

Put in a microwave bowl, tightly cover with clingwrap and cook on high for 5–6 minutes until soft. Then strain in a fine sieve and puree in a blender.

'The origins of the microwave are fascinating. In 1945 Percy Le Baron Spencer, an American engineer, was standing next to a magnetron (a piece of equipment which drives a radar) when the chocolate bar in his pocket began to melt. After subsequent experiments with popping corn and exploding eggs he realised that microwave radio signals could cook food. Under the name Radarange he created the first experimental microwave which was six feet tall and weighed 750 pounds. Commercial ovens were released on the market three years later and in 1967 his company, Raytheon, introduced the first countertop microwave.'

Cinnamon-Thyme Tea

1 bunch thyme
8 cups water
4 whole cinnamon sticks
2 slices of fresh lemon

Put in a large pot, slightly cover and simmer for about 20 minutes until liquid has reduced to about 5 cups. Strain and serve.

'A restorative.'

Moroccan Mint Tea

2 tspn Chinese green tea
1 tbsp chopped fresh spearmint

Rinse a teapot with boiling water. Then add tea and mint to pot.

900 ml boiling water

Pour into pot and leave to stand for 5 minutes.

sugar to taste
lemon slices
small sprigs of mint

Pour tea through a strainer into cups, add sugar and lemon to taste (it should be fairly sweet) and garnish with mint.

'In Morocco, mint tea is offered to anyone who visits as a sign of hospitality. Tea arrived in Morocco in 1854 when, during the Crimean War, the blockade of the Baltic forced British merchants to find new markets.'

Chilli Infused Oil

(MAKES 750 ML)

15 small dried chillies	Soak in warm water for 10 minutes. Then drain well and roughly chop.
750 ml olive oil 2 bay leaves 6 sprigs of rosemary	Heat, along with chillies, over the lowest possible heat for 30 minutes. Then cool and strain well.
3 fresh chillies 2 long rosemary stalks	Put in a bottle and pour oil over the top.

Basil Infused Oil

(MAKES 750 ML)

5 cups tightly packed fresh, unblemished basil leaves	Add to a large pot of boiling water and push under surface. Cook for 5 seconds, strain and run under cold tap. Then drain very well and, with your hands, squeeze out any liquid.
750 ml olive oil	Whiz up in a blender with basil and then strain through 4 layers of cheesecloth. Tightly cover, and store in refrigerator. Use within 1 week.

'Infused oils are wonderful with bread, added to dressings or sauces or simply sprinkled over grilled meat, poultry or seafood. And, using these guidelines, experiment with different flavours – for example, instead of chillies add rinds of parmesan to just bubbling oil.'

Preserved Lemons

8–10 lemons
250 g kitchen salt

Scrub lemons well and cut into quarters. Place in a large bowl, add salt and mix very well.

lemon juice

Pack into a sterilised preserving jar, adding salt layer by layer and pressing on lemons as you add. Then add extra lemon juice to almost cover and firmly press down on lemons. Seal and leave for 1 month before using, turning the jar every now and then.

'These lemons will keep for at least 3 or 4 months in the refrigerator.'

Italian Sweet & Sour Onions • Sybil's Cabbage & Gherkin Slaw • Creamed Spinach

Lemon Rice (in the Rice Cooker) • Cabbage & Bacon Salad • Braised Celeriac • Celeriac Remoulade •

Green Bean Salad with Pesto Bean, Fetta & Mint Salad • Roasted Beetroot Salad with

Spiced Yoghurt • Creamed Brussels Sprouts • BBQ Potatoes with Lemon & Chive Dressing • Beetroot Chips

Pumpkin with Soy & Honey Caramel • Baked Baby Spuds in Foil • Rosemary & Garlic Baby Potatoes •

Champ (Irish Mashed Potatoes) • Claypot Potatoes with Bacon & Chive Cream • Crispy, Crunchy Roast

Potatoes • Oven-Baked Potato Wedges • Parsnip Gratin • Fennel & Parmesan Gratin

Italian Rice Salad • Citrus Couscous

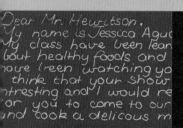

Dear Mr. Hewitson,
My name is Jessica Agua
My class have been lear
bout healthy foods and
have been watching yo
think that your show
ntresting and I would re
or you to come to our
nd cook a delicous m

On the Side

Although in many cases I whip up dishes that involve vegies in a reasonably major role, it is also nice to present something a little special in the middle of the table.

Of course, there is also the case of plainer grills and sautés which definitely need a reasonably fancy accompaniment.

And, there are days when, for no reason at all, I just throw in one of these dishes purely and simply because they taste good.

Italian Sweet & Sour Onions

(SERVES 4)

30 baby onions, peeled (see below)
1 tbsp olive oil
1 tbsp balsamic vinegar
2 tbsp brown sugar
$^1/_2$ cup vegetable stock, bought or homemade
   (see page 198)
freshly ground salt & pepper

chopped fresh parsley

Preheat oven to 180°C.
Put onions in a baking dish just large enough to hold them. Pour over stock and sprinkle with rest of ingredients. Cook for about 1 hour until onions are tender, tossing every now and again (and adding a little more stock to pan if necessary).

Serve in a flat bowl with all juices and parsley over the top.

'To peel baby onions, put them in a deep bowl and pour in boiling water to cover. Peel when cool enough to handle.'

Sybil's Cabbage & Gherkin Slaw

(SERVES 4)

$\frac{1}{2}$ small savoy cabbage, cleaned & core removed	Finely slice, discarding ribs.
3 gherkins, chopped 3 hard boiled eggs, chopped 2 tbsp chopped fresh parsley juice of 1 lemon freshly ground salt & pepper	Add to cabbage, mix and set aside for 30 minutes.
4–6 tbsp mayonnaise, bought or homemade (see page 23) chopped fresh parsley	Add mayonnaise and mix in well. Put in a bowl and sprinkle with parsley.

'A restaurant meal was hardly a restaurant meal, in my early days, unless every dish was accompanied by a pile of coleslaw (and a slice of orange along with a normally tired wedge of tomato). This would have been fine if only the slaw had been of this standard – unfortunately this was rarely the case.'

Creamed Spinach

(SERVES 4)

table salt
4 good handfuls of baby spinach, well
  washed

Blanch spinach in plenty of lightly salted boiling water until just wilted. Then drain, run under cold water and drain in colander for 10 minutes.

a good knob of butter
$^1/_2$ tspn plain flour
3 tbsp cream
a pinch of nutmeg
freshly ground salt & pepper

Squeeze any liquid out of spinach with your hands and finely chop. Then heat butter in a pan, add spinach and toss. Add flour, turn down heat and cook for 1 minute. Add cream, nutmeg and seasonings and cook until thickened.

'Creamed spinach was a very popular accompaniment when I first began working in restaurants. I know, because I was the poor bugger who had to wash the tonnes of spinach every day. Because, as you know, cooked spinach almost disappears to nothing.'

Lemon Rice (in the Rice Cooker)

(SERVES 4–6)

2 cups basmati rice	Put in a bowl and put under cold running water. Leave until water runs clear and then drain.
olive oil spray	Spray a little on bottom of a rice cooker bowl and put drained rice in.
2$\frac{1}{2}$ cups chicken stock, bought or homemade (see page 62) good pinch of salt	Add and mix well. Cover, turn on and cook until machine turns to warm.
$\frac{1}{2}$ tbsp finely grated lemon zest 4 tbsp butter 4 tbsp chopped fresh parsley	Add, stir to combine. Cover and leave for 10 minutes. Then fluff up with a fork.

'Stop thinking of your rice cooker as one dimensional – start thinking of different additions, flavourings and even main course one pot (or should that be onecooker) numbers.'

Cabbage & Bacon Salad

(SERVES 6–8)

1 small savoy cabbage, core & ribs removed
   & finely sliced

Put in a bowl and pour boiling water over the top. Leave for 10 minutes and then drain well.

3 tbsp olive oil
3 bacon rashers, rindless & finely sliced
2 tbsp red wine vinegar
2 tbsp chopped fresh parsley
freshly ground salt & pepper

Heat oil in a pan and sauté bacon. When crispy, add vinegar and parsley, swirl and pour over drained cabbage. Toss well, adding a little more oil if necessary and seasonings to taste.

'When buying cabbage, choose compact, heavy ones with crisp leaves free of slime or insect holes. And, unless you intend to use them straight away, buy whole ones because cut edges give off enzymes that cause them to deteriorate.'

Hi Hewy – Baby!

We now have a Huey's meal at least five times a week. Sometimes I nearly take my husband's breath away with the slurp of chilli paste. But we've never had such a variety of meals – I had never used chilli before or many of your herbs. We have a pantry full now and I am trying to grow coriander. We lived in Canada 40 years ago and we absolutely adored their Western Omelettes. I have tried and tried to duplicate them to no avail. Can you please help me?
Wilma VIC

How good it is to see a cooking show that ordinary folk can understand. I am 72, had a large family and lived mostly on a farm as I do now. I learnt to cook via my gran during wartime so learnt to do with what we had. I have never really measured, just thrown things together so it's hard when someone asks for a recipe! I do have plenty of cookbooks but I honestly hardly use them. I try to get in for your show though, it gives me a spell from my chores.
Kathleen WA

I am self-taught and like your splash and dash ways. I think that all your show needs is an offsider to throw in the odd comment and banter. I would like to apply for that position as I can cook and I have a big mouth and with my sense of humour thrown in alongside yours it could be a winning combination. The ABC had Two Fat Ladies. We could be the Huey and Suey Show.
Susanne NSW

Braised Celeriac

(SERVES 4)

$^{1}/_{2}$ garlic clove, crushed
2–3 celeriac, peeled & sliced
1 cup chicken stock, bought or homemade
   (see page 62)
freshly ground salt & pepper
2 tbsp butter
2 tbsp chopped fresh parsley

Smear garlic in the base of a pot. Add rest of ingredients and gently simmer for 10–12 minutes until just tender.

Celeriac Remoulade

(SERVES 4)

4 tbsp mayonnaise, bought or homemade
   (see page 23)
3 tbsp sour cream
1 heaped tspn Dijon mustard
1 tbsp chopped fresh parsley

Mix together.

2 celeriac, peeled & coarsely grated
fresh lemon juice

Add and mix in with lemon juice to taste.

'Celeriac, a type of celery, is a delicious vegie, but unlike normal celery only the root is eaten. When preparing in advance, always cover with water along with a squeeze of lemon juice as the flesh quickly discolours on contact with air.'

Green Bean Salad with Pesto

(SERVES 4)

table salt 3–4 dozen small green beans, topped & tailed	Blanch in plenty of lightly salted boiling water until crisp-tender and drain well.
pesto, bought or homemade (see page 42) freshly ground salt & pepper fresh parmesan shavings	Toss with pesto and seasonings to taste. Put in a bowl and scatter parmesan on top.

Bean, Fetta & Mint Salad

(SERVES 4)

table salt 3–4 dozen small green beans, topped & tailed	Blanch in plenty of lightly salted boiling water until crisp-tender and drain well.
6 pitted black olives, sliced 100 g fetta cheese, crumbled 8 sliced fresh mint leaves freshly ground salt & pepper extra virgin olive oil balsamic vinegar	Toss with olives, fetta and mint along with seasonings, oil and vinegar to taste.

'There is only one secret when boiling green vegies – plenty of rapidly boiling water. Because the sooner it comes back to the boil the more the vegies flavour will be sealed in (so I suppose I better add another rule – don't overcrowd the pot.)'

Roasted Beetroot Salad with Spiced Yoghurt

(SERVES 4)

4–6 medium beetroot, well scrubbed

Preheat oven to 200°C.
Individually wrap in foil and cook in oven for about 55 minutes until tender when pierced with a small, sharp knife. Unwrap and leave until cool enough to handle.

a squeeze of fresh lemon juice
olive oil
freshly ground salt & pepper

Then peel beetroot (see below) and cut into wedges. While still hot, toss with lemon juice, a little oil and seasonings. Put in a bowl.

3 heaped tbsp yoghurt
a pinch of ground cumin
a pinch of ground coriander
1 tbsp chopped coriander
a good squeeze of fresh lemon

Mix together and mound on top of beetroot. Serve hot or at room temperature as an accompaniment to any grill or as part of an antipasto selection.

'To peel beetroot, put your rubber gloves on and peel under running water.'

Creamed Brussels Sprouts

(SERVES 4)

table salt
15–20 brussels sprouts, damaged & outer
    leaves removed

Blanch in a large pot of lightly salted boiling water for a few minutes. Then drain and, when cool enough to handle, coarsely chop.

2–3 tbsp butter
freshly ground salt & pepper
$1/4$ cup cream
2 tbsp chopped fresh parsley

Melt butter in a pot, add sprouts and toss well. Season and add cream and parsley. Gently cook for 4–5 minutes, regularly stirring. Taste for seasoning.

'I think that even avid haters of brussels sprouts will enjoy this dish (but maybe I'm just kidding myself).'

BBQ Potatoes with Lemon & Chive Dressing
(SERVES 4)

6 large potatoes, well scrubbed & boiled until
   just tender
vegetable oil
freshly ground salt & pepper

Preheat BBQ or grill.
Cut spuds into thick slices and season.
Lightly oil grill, put potatoes on and cook
turning and brushing with oil as you do so.

6 tbsp olive oil
juice of 1 lemon
1 heaped tbsp Dijon mustard
2 tbsp snipped fresh chives

Whisk together and, when potatoes are
cooked, put in a flat bowl and sprinkle
dressing over the top.

'The potato which is, these days, about our most popular vegie had, at first, a hard time being accepted (that is apart from Ireland where they were supposedly first planted by Sir Walter Raleigh in the 1500's and instantly became an overnight success). But in Spain they were regarded as tasteless and only suitable for the poor, while in France (before Parmentier, see page 140) they weren't even good enough for the poor and were fed strictly to the animals. As well, Scotland's Presbyterian ministers declared that they were unholy because they didn't happen to be mentioned in the Bible and English politicians hardly bothered with them, except to dismiss them as 'Ireland's lazy root', whatever that means.'

Beetroot Chips

(SERVES 4)

6 cups vegetable oil	Heat to 180°–190°C (see page 15).
4–6 medium beetroot, peeled & finely sliced (using a bench slicer or mandolin)	Drop into a bowl of iced water. Then drain and dry well. Deep-fry in batches, keeping separate. When cooked, drain well on paper towels. (They will be soft at first, but will crisp up after a few minutes.)

'Beetroot (or any root vegetable) chips are a great accompaniment to a drink or two.'

Pumpkin with Soy & Honey Caramel

(SERVES 4)

top half of a butternut pumpkin, peeled	Preheat BBQ or grill Cut into even slices about $\frac{1}{2}$ cm thick.
olive oil 2 heaped tbsp honey 2 heaped tbsp soy sauce	Toss with a little oil and cook, regularly turning. When almost done, mix together honey and soy and generously brush on and continue doing so until caramelised.
chopped fresh parsley	Sprinkle with a little parsley.

'Delicious.'

Rosemary & Garlic Baby Potatoes

(SERVES 4)

12–16 baby spuds, well washed & cut in half
6–8 whole garlic cloves, unpeeled & flattened
   a little with a kitchen knife
olive oil
sprigs from 2 stalks of rosemary
freshly ground salt & pepper

Preheat oven to 230°C.
Place in a bowl with a little oil and toss well.
Then spread onto a tray and cook in oven
for about 30 minutes until spuds are crisp,
golden and tender.

Baked Baby Spuds in Foil

(SERVES 4)

12–16 baby spuds, well washed

Preheat oven to 250°C.
Blanch in lightly salted boiling water until
just tender and drain well.

olive oil
2–3 spring (green) onions, chopped
freshly ground salt & pepper
butter

Oil 4 squares of kitchen foil. Then top with
potatoes, spring onions, seasonings and a
knob of butter. Tightly wrap up and cook
in oven for 10–12 minutes.

'Friedrich Wilhelm Nietzsche wrote that 'a diet that
consists predominantly of rice leads to the use of opium,
just as a diet that consists predominantly of potatoes
leads to the use of liquor' – I must keep that in mind.'

Champ (Irish Mashed Potatoes)

(SERVES 4–8)

table salt 1 kg potatoes, peeled & chopped	Cook in lightly salted boiling water until tender and drain.
$^1/_2$ cup chopped spring (green) onions $^1/_4$ cup milk $^1/_4$ cup cream	Bring to the boil and then mash potatoes, adding this mix little by little as you do so.
soft butter freshly ground salt & pepper	Add a good dollop of butter and season to taste.
extra soft butter	To serve, top with a generous dollop of butter.

'Traditionally, champ is eaten from the outside in, dipping each forkful into the butter. And while we are on the subject of mash, why not try adding other flavours such as pesto (see page 42), black olive paste or even roasted garlic (see page 2).'

Claypot Potatoes with Bacon & Chive Cream

(SERVES 6–8)

1cm thick piece of rindless bacon, cut in 3
20 baby potatoes, well scrubbed
freshly ground salt & pepper

sour cream
snipped fresh chives

Preheat oven to 220°C.
Put bacon in a claypot, top with spuds and seasonings. Put cover on and cook for 1 hour.

Put spuds in a bowl. Slice bacon and add along with cooking juices. Toss well and top with a good dollop of sour cream and chives.

'If bacon is not to your liking put a layer of sea salt in the base of the claypot instead. Then cook as above just remembering, when you serve, to brush any salt off first with a pastry brush.'

Oven-Baked Potato Wedges

(SERVES 4)

table salt
4 large potatoes, well scrubbed

Preheat oven to 220°C.
Cook in lightly salted boiling water until tender. Then cool and cut into wedges.

olive oil
freshly ground salt

Place wedges on an oiled baking sheet, brush with oil and sprinkle with salt. Cook in oven until golden and crisp, turning once.

'You most probably thought you would never hear me say this, but the potatoes should be a bit overcooked so that they have all those rough edges which will end up extra crispy and crunchy.'

Crispy, Crunchy Roast Potatoes

table salt
medium–large potatoes, peeled & cut in 4

Cook in lightly salted boiling water for 5 minutes.

olive oil
freshly ground salt & pepper

Allow to cool and then scrape all surfaces with the prongs of a fork. Toss with oil and seasonings and cook in oven until crispy and crunchy.

'The rough edges, in a similar vein to the Oven-Baked Potato Wedges, are what makes these crispy and crunchy.'

Parsnip Gratin

(SERVES 4–6)

table salt	Preheat oven to 220°C.
8 medium parsnips, peeled	Blanch in a large pot of lightly salted boiling water until just tender. Drain, cool a little and slice.
grated tasty cheese	Layer parsnips in a gratin dish with cheese,
freshly ground salt & pepper	seasonings and a sprinkling of cream
cream	and parsley, finishing with a cheese and
chopped fresh parsley	cream layer. Cook in oven for about 10–15 minutes until golden brown.

Fennel & Parmesan Gratin

(SERVES 4–6)

8 small fennel bulbs	Preheat oven to 220°C.
table salt	Cut in half lengthways. Then blanch in lightly salted boiling water until crisp-tender and drain well.
2 garlic cloves, crushed	Smear garlic in the base of a gratin dish.
chicken stock, bought or homemade (see page 62)	Lay half of fennel on top and sprinkle with stock, seasonings and cheese. Repeat and
freshly ground salt & pepper	cook for about 20 minutes until bubbling.
freshly grated parmesan	

 'Two very underrated vegies which deserve another moment in the spotlight – particularly in this manner where they are wonderful accompaniments to everything from a roast leg of lamb or chook, to the family barbie.'

Italian Rice Salad

(SERVES 4)

1 cup arborio rice

2 cups chicken stock, bought or homemade
   (see page 62)

3 tbsp pesto, bought or homemade
   (see page 42)

Put in a large pot, mix well, tightly cover
and simmer for 20 minutes.

2 tbsp freshly grated parmesan

a squeeze of fresh lemon juice

extra pesto to taste

Put rice in a bowl, add and mix well.

Citrus Couscous

(SERVES 4)

1 cup orange juice

1 tspn ground cinnamon

2 tbsp olive oil

1 cup couscous

1 tbsp sliced preserved lemon, bought
   or homemade (see page 226)

2 tbsp raisins

a dollop of soft butter

Bring orange juice, cinnamon and oil to the
boil. Pour over couscous, lemon and raisins
and mix in well. Leave for 3 minutes until
swollen then stir in butter and fluff with a
fork. (This can be done in advance and
reheated in the microwave.)

Apple & Rhubarb Crumble • Baptist Apple Cake • Greek Berry Pudding • Sticky Date Pudding • Mars Bar

Apples • Quince & Apple Cobbler • Cam's Chocolate Mud Cake • Strawberries with Balsamic

Strawberry Bruschetta • Italian Rhubarb Trifle • Coconut Ice • Chocolate Salami • Chocky Cornflake

Crackles • Rice Bubble & Coco Pop Slice • Chocolate Honey Mousse • Claudia Roden's Middle Eastern

Orange & Almond Cake  Bread & Butter Pudding • White Chocolate Moussecake • Pavlova •

Strawberry & Orange Mascarpone Tart • Fresh Fruit Salad with a Lemon Jelly • Tea-Poached Dates •

Lumberjack Cake • Poached Fresh Pears with Lemon Ricotta and a Honey & Passionfruit Sauce • Chocolate

& Ginger Ice Box Cake 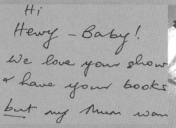 Italian Rice Pudding • Xmas Ice-Cream Pudding

Hi
Hewy – Baby!
We love your show
& have your books
but my mum wan

Sweet Tooth

I am actually not the greatest fan of desserts – in fact that's not quite true –
I don't mind eating the blessed things, but I'm not really that keen on cooking
them. I think it's all that measuring stuff that gets to me because, as you may
have noticed, I'm more of a handful-of-this, and a splash-of-that type of guy.

That said, there is nothing more satisfying than producing a perfect cake, tart
or pastry – rising in the right places, moist where necessary and, above all,
watching as it is eagerly devoured by your guests. And, to be honest, desserts
(particularly those involving chocolate) are amongst our most requested recipes.
So, whether I like it or not, the odd dessert or pastry has emanated from the
Hewitson oven. But, you know what, I still don't like all that measuring stuff
(and I actually did have one abject failure when I ignored all the rules and a
lemon cake, instead of rising, deflated rather alarmingly and ended up as a
decidedly rubbery pancake type affair).

Apple & Rhubarb Crumble
(SERVES 6–8)

6 medium Granny Smith apples, peeled,
   cored & chopped
8 rhubarb stalks, leaves removed, washed &
   then chopped
$^1/_2$ cup brown sugar
juice of 1 orange
juice of 1 lemon

Preheat oven to 180°C.
Place in a pot and simmer for 10 minutes until soft. Mix well and put in a deep oven dish.

$^3/_4$ cup rolled oats
$^3/_4$ cup plain flour
100 g brown sugar
1 tspn ground ginger
80–100 g unsalted butter, melted
1 tspn baking powder

Mix together, spread over the top and cook in oven for 40 minutes until topping is golden brown.

'You can use almost any fruit for a crumble, but in our household they were normally made with apples or rhubarb or, as in this case, a combination of both.'

Baptist Apple Cake

{SERVES 6–8}

3 Granny Smith apples, peeled, cored & chopped 1 cup raw sugar 115 g unsalted butter, melted 1 egg 1^1/$_2$ cups plain flour	Preheat oven to 180°C. Combine.
1 tspn baking powder 2 tspn cinnamon ^{1}/$_2$ tspn nutmeg ^{1}/$_2$ tspn mixed spice	Add and mix well. Put into a greased, round 20 cm cake tin and smooth out.
^{1}/$_2$ cup brown sugar ^{1}/$_2$ cup rolled oats 1 tspn cinnamon 30 g unsalted butter, melted	Combine, sprinkle on top of cake and cook in oven for 40–45 minutes until a skewer comes out clean. Serve warm or cold with lightly whipped cream.

'This came from a New Zealand newspaper column. It is a delightful cake but, sadly, there was no explanation as to why it is called a 'Baptist' Apple Cake.'

Greek Berry Pudding

(SERVES 6–8)

1 cup cream, lightly whipped 500 g Greek-style yoghurt 2 tbsp honey	Combine in a bowl.
4 cups mixed berries, hulled & washed	Evenly spread in a bowl or gratin dish and top with the yoghurt mix.
soft brown sugar	Sprinkle with a generous amount of sugar, cover with kitchen wrap and refrigerate for at least 2 hours.

'I have tried this with a fruit flavoured yoghurt. This works well, as does good old fashioned fresh fruit salad instead of the berries.'

Sticky Date Pudding

(SERVES 8–10)

170 g dates, pitted & sliced	Preheat oven to 160°C.
300 ml water	Put into a pot and bring to the boil.
1 tspn bicarb soda	Remove from the heat and add.
60 g unsalted butter	Then cream butter and sugar. Add eggs, one
170 g caster sugar	at a time, beating well after each addition.
2 eggs	Gently fold in flour and then stir in dates and
170 g self-raising flour	vanilla. Pour into a buttered 20 cm round
¹/₂ tspn vanilla essence	cake tin and cook in oven for 30–40 minutes
	until a skewer comes out clean.
200 g brown sugar	Put in a pot, bring to the boil and simmer for
130 g unsalted butter	3 minutes. Pour a little over the pudding and
¹/₂ cup cream	return to the oven for 2–3 minutes.
¹/₂ tspn vanilla essence	
lightly whipped cream	Serve in wedges with cream and remaining
	sauce on the side.

'This highly popular dessert came from English food magazine **A La Carte** via Sydney chef Annie Parmentier who first featured it on her Sydney restaurant menu (where it quickly became an overnight success with both customers and fellow chefs alike).'

Mars Bar Apples

(SERVES 4)

4 Granny Smith apples, cored
1–2 Mars Bars
muscat

Preheat BBQ (or oven to 210°C).
Slice Mars Bars and stuff into the centre of
apples. Put on squares of foil, generously
sprinkle with muscat (or port) and tightly
wrap up.

lightly whipped cream

Cook for 25–30 minutes, then unwrap and
serve with all juices poured over the top
and a dollop of cream.

'Not content with taking me to the Flower Drum for sweet & sour pork,
my mate Bob Hart also came up with this recipe. I sneered but then had
to admit the stuffed apples were decidedly more-ish.'

Quince & Apple Cobbler

(SERVES 6–8)

1 kg quinces, peeled, cored & sliced 1^{1}/$_{2}$ cups sugar 3 cups water	Put in a pot and simmer, partially covered, for about 30 minutes until tender.
750 g Granny Smith apples, peeled, cored & sliced	Add and cook at a rapid boil until apples are tender. Drain a little, if necessary, and put in an oven or gratin dish.
^{1}/$_{4}$ cup sugar 1 egg	Preheat oven to 180°C. Beat until thick.
1 cup plain flour 1 tbsp baking powder 1 tbsp vanilla extract ^{1}/$_{2}$ cup milk	Add to above and whisk well until smooth. Pour over quince mix and cook in oven for about 35–40 minutes until golden.
icing sugar lightly whipped cream	Dust with icing sugar and serve with cream on the side.

'The quince is an old-fashioned fruit that we tend to ignore. Which is a shame because this is a delicious, perfumed number, not only wonderful in crumbles, pies and cobblers but it makes the most superb jellies and jams. (And let us not forget quince paste which is a brilliant accompaniment to a well-aged cheddar cheese.)'

Cam's Chocolate Mud Cake

(SERVES 10–12)

250 g unsalted butter, diced	Preheat oven to 160°–170°C.
2 cups caster sugar	Put in a bowl and put over simmering
150 g dark cooking chocolate	water. Cook very slowly for 10–15 minutes,
$^1/_3$ cup whisky or brandy	stirring every few minutes or so until
1 heaped tbsp instant coffee	chocolate is melted.
1 cup hot water	
$1^1/_2$ cups plain flour	Sift into another large bowl and gently
$^1/_4$ cup self–raising flour	whisk a third of the chocolate mix in.
$^1/_4$ cup cocoa	Continue adding chocolate mix little by
	little and mix until smooth.
2 eggs	Gently mix in (be careful not to form air
	pockets).
	Pour into a lightly greased 20 cm
	springform cake tin and place a circle of
	baking paper on top. Put on middle rung of
	oven over a tray of hot water and cook for
	about 1 hour 20 minutes until just cooked
	when tested with a skewer. Cool on a rack.
250 g dark cooking chocolate	Place in a pot and cook until smooth,
200 ml cream	regularly stirring. Then cool a little and
	pour over cake.

'Another very popular number from Tolarno pastry chef Cameron Cox.'

Strawberries with Balsamic

(serves 4)

2 punnets of strawberries, hulled & washed
2 tbsp caster sugar

Toss strawberries in sugar and leave for 30 minutes.

2 tbsp balsamic vinegar
icing sugar
mint sprigs

Gently toss with balsamic and, to serve, place in glasses, sprinkle with icing sugar and garnish with mint.

Strawberry Bruschetta

(SERVES 4)

4 slices country-style bread, thickly sliced

Preheat overhead grill and toast on one side.

2 punnets of strawberries, hulled & thickly sliced
caster sugar

Pile on untoasted side of bread, sprinkle with sugar and grill.

mascarpone cheese
icing sugar
mint sprigs

Top with a scoop of mascarpone, dust with icing sugar and garnish with mint.

'I stole this ripper idea from bills in Sydney (although I don't think they add mascarpone). I have made it with other fruit such as apples, figs and kiwi fruit, also with great success.'

Italian Rhubarb Trifle

(SERVES 4)

1 bunch of rhubarb, leaves discarded, washed
   & cut in lengths
1 cup orange juice
2 tbsp brown sugar

Put in a pot and add water to just cover. Cook until tender and then drain. Put in a bowl and mix in a little cooking liquid.

1 cup strong coffee, cold
3 tbsp brandy
4 tbsp Frangelico
1 stale sponge, bought or homemade, cubed

In another bowl, mix together coffee, brandy and Frangelico. Add sponge cubes and toss until well coated.

1 cup mascarpone
1 tbsp Frangelico
2 tspn caster sugar
1 cup cream, whipped

Mix together mascarpone, Frangelico and sugar. Then fold in cream.

Dutch cocoa

Place rhubarb in the bottom of a bowl or gratin dish. Top with sponge and then mascarpone cream. Smooth, dust with cocoa and refrigerate until ready to serve.

'The cheat's tiramisu.'

Dear Huey...

>As a fellow Kiwi I wanted to
thank you for cooking coconut
ice on your show. I haven't had
it since I was a kid. So I
thought I'd pass on a tip my
mother used whenever she made it
- she put blobs of the mixture
(white first then pink) into the
tin, covered it with Gladwrap
then pressed it out to the edges
using a block of butter or copha
from the fridge. You get a
perfect result without the
sticky fingers.
Caroline QLD

>For some time I have been after a recipe for a Greek
dish called Deep Fried Pumpkin Scones. They have
sultanas in them and are served with a warm syrup.
They are reputed to be an aphrodisiac, but as my
girlfriend has said on many occasions they are
actually BTS (better than sex). Hope you can help
me out. They really are divine.
Imelda NSW

>Watching you grapple with the yellow food colouring
for the lemon sauce last week, my Nan showed me a tip
once when preparing coloured icing. She used a small
metal skewer which can be dipped in the bottle as
shallow or as deep as required. It works every time
and brings back many happy memories of cooking with
her in the kitchen.
Lesley

>Just once I'd like to see you NOT clean up the plate
. . . is that possible? Every day I find myself
hoping and praying you won't spill any on the sides
of the plate, but I suppose you're not perfect.
Jen

Coconut Ice

(SERVES 8–12)

180 g copha	Slowly melt in a pot.
750 g icing sugar	Sieve icing sugar into a bowl and combine
375 g desiccated coconut	with coconut.
$1^1/_2$ tspn vanilla essence	Add and, once again, combine well. Then
$^3/_4$ tspn fresh lemon juice	add copha and mix. Divide mixture in two
3 egg whites, lightly beaten	and press half into a sprayed cookie tin.
cooking spray	
cochineal (red food dye)	Add a few drops to remaining mix,
	combine well and press on top. Then cover
	with greaseproof paper and refrigerate for
	20 minutes. Cut into squares and serve.

'One of the most popular items at my restaurant Tolarno. The only problem is that the staff (including me) tend to scoff the lot.'

Chocolate Salami

(SERVES 4)

300 g caster sugar
125 ml water

Put in a pot and boil for 5 minutes, then place in a bowl.

375 g unsalted pistachios, chopped

Add, mix well and cool for a few minutes.

175 g Dutch cocoa
125 g slightly soft, unsalted butter, cubed
2 eggs
50 g cream

Add and mix well. Then put a large piece of foil on bench, place mixture down centre and roll, squeezing both ends tightly like a bonbon to ensure that it is round.

icing sugar

Put on a baking tray and freeze overnight. To serve, unwrap, slice and dust with icing sugar.

'This came from a former sous chef Janis Munro who got the recipe from Annie Smithers who, in turn, got the recipe (I think) from Stephanie Alexander.'

Chocky Cornflake Crackles

(MAKES ABOUT 12)

475 g dark cooking chocolate	Put in a bowl and melt over simmering water.
4$\frac{1}{2}$ cups cornflakes	Place in a large bowl, pour over half of the chocolate and gently mix with a rubber spatula. Then add rest of chocolate and continue to gently mix until well coated. Drop spoonfuls into paper patty cases and refrigerate until set.

'This recipe was a huge hit — I prepared it with the Wiggles at a children's playground and, although there wasn't a refrigerator in sight (to set them), they disappeared as fast as we could make them.'

Rice Bubble & Coco Pop Slice

(SERVES 6–8)

140 g honey
110 g caster sugar
125 g unsalted butter
80 g smooth peanut butter

Place in a pot and gently cook until sugar has dissolved and the butter has melted. Then boil for 5 minutes without stirring.

cooking spray
baking paper

Lightly spray a cookie tin, 30 cm x 20 cm, place baking paper on base and spray again.

90 g Coco Pops
75 g Rice Bubbles
1 cup shredded coconut

Put in a bowl, add hot mix and combine well until dry ingredients are well coated. Then press evenly into tin and refrigerate for at least 3 hours. Cut into squares to serve.

'A favourite with kids of all ages, this recipe is an oldie from the **Australian Women's Weekly**.'

Chocolate Honey Mousse

(SERVES 4)

350 g dark cooking chocolate ³/₄ cup cream 4 generous tbsp honey	Put in a bowl and melt over simmering water until smooth, regularly mixing. Cool a little.
2¹/₄ cups cream	Whip until soft peaks form and then fold chocolate mix through, little by little. Put in a large bowl or individual ones and refrigerate for at least 3 hours.

'Any dessert with chocolate involved is invariably popular. In fact, so much so, that I reckon if I whipped up that African favourite, chocolate coated ants, the recipe requests would still flood in (maybe next year).'

Claudia Roden's Middle Eastern Orange & Almond Cake

(SERVES 8–10)

2 large oranges, washed

Cook in plenty of boiling water for 2 hours, adding more water if necessary. Then coarsely chop, including skin, and remove any pips.

6 eggs, beaten
250 g ground almonds
250 g sugar
1 tspn baking powder

Preheat oven to 190°C.
Put in a processor along with oranges and any juice. Then whiz until thoroughly mixed.

cooking spray

Spray a 20 cm springform cake tin, pour in batter and cook in oven for 1 hour. Check with skewer and, if still wet, cook a little longer. Cool in tin before turning out onto a cake rack.

'Ms Roden just dusts this terrific, moist cake with icing sugar. Which is fine. But I also like it topped with an orange icing which I make by whisking until smooth 2 cups icing sugar, 1 tablespoon orange liqueur, 1 tablespoon fresh orange juice, 1 tablespoon melted unsalted butter and 1 tablespoon chopped mixed citrus peel. Then warm over a double boiler until it melts a little before spreading over the cake.

Bread & Butter Pudding

(SERVES 6–8)

8 tbsp dried apricots, chopped
4 tbsp golden raisins
whisky

Preheat oven to 160°C.
Put fruit in a bowl, cover with whisky and set aside to soak for 15 minutes or so.

soft unsalted butter
4–6 bread rolls

Butter a large oval or square gratin dish, place fruit in bottom and sprinkle with all the juices. Then thickly slice rolls, butter on both sides and place in dish to about four fifths of the way up.

250 ml milk
250 ml thick cream
1 vanilla bean, split
3 large eggs
125 g caster sugar

Bring milk, cream and vanilla to the boil. At the same time, whisk eggs and sugar in a mixer until thick and pale. Then, continually whisking, add milk and cream mix. Strain and carefully pour over bread.

Place a sheet of folded newspaper in a deep baking dish (this stops the pudding catching), place pudding on top and add enough boiling water to come halfway up the side. Cook in oven for 40–45 minutes until risen and golden, yet still wobbly in the centre.

3 tbsp apricot jam
icing sugar

Melt jam over a low heat with a little water and then paint on top of the pudding and dust with icing sugar.

'This recipe is a bit of a mixture from two of London's finest chefs, Richard Shepherd and Anton Mosimann.'

White Chocolate Moussecake

(SERVES 8–10)

125 g plain chocolate biscuits 60 g unsalted butter, melted 1/2 tspn ground cinnamon	Crumble biscuits in a processor and then mix together with butter and cinnamon.
cooking spray	Spray base and sides of a 20 cm round springform cake tin and press biscuit mix into base.
400 g white chocolate	Melt over simmering water.
50 g dried apricots, chopped 50 g glace cherries, chopped 50 g crystallised pineapple, chopped 50 g flaked almonds, toasted 1/4 cup white rum	Soak fruit and nuts in rum.
4 egg yolks 30 ml cream 30 ml white rum 1/2 tbsp orange flower water grated zest of 1 orange	Beat, with a hand-held electric beater, until well mixed.
3 tbsp powdered gelatine 4 tbsp boiling water 40 g liquid glucose 2 cups cream, lightly whipped	Dissolve gelatine in water, add glucose and briefly beat into egg mix. Then fold in chocolate, fruit and whipped cream. Pour into tin and refrigerate for 2–3 hours until set.

'A very classy little number.'

Pavlova

(SERVES 8–10)

6 fresh egg whites

Preheat oven to 140°–150°C.
Beat in a very clean, dry bowl for about
5–6 minutes until stiff peaks form.

500 g caster sugar

Then while continually beating, add one
tbsp at a time until fully incorporated.

$\frac{1}{2}$ tbsp cornflour
$\frac{1}{2}$ tbsp white vinegar
$\frac{1}{2}$ tbsp vanilla essence

Combine and slowly pour into meringue,
whisking until stiff peaks re-form.

baking paper
icing sugar

Line a baking tray with paper and dust with
icing sugar. Then place meringue in the
centre and shape with a plastic spatula,
making sure edges are straight. Cook in
oven for 40–50 minutes until crispish on
outside and some cracks appear on surface.
Allow to cool.

whipped cream
passionfruit pulp
fresh fruit, such as strawberries & kiwifruit

Generously spread with cream and garnish
with fruit.

'This began life as my Auntie Peggy's recipe. My mother then added her
variations and, more recently, Cam added a few of his own.'

Strawberry & Orange Mascarpone Tart

(SERVES 4–6)

1 bought puff pastry sheet	Preheat oven to 170°C. Put pastry on a baking sheet and prick all over with a fork. Then cook in oven for 8–10 minutes, gently flatten with a clean tea towel and turn over. Cook for another 5 minutes and cool on a cake rack.
1 cup mascarpone grated rind & juice of 1 orange a good splash orange liqueur	Mix together, adding more liqueur and juice if necessary.
2 punnets of strawberries, hulled orange liqueur	Toss strawberries with a good splash of liqueur.
icing sugar	When pastry is cool, put a layer of mascarpone on top and then strawberries. Dust with icing sugar.

'This tart/sweet cheese filling is a great substitute for the more traditional crème patisserie.'

Fresh Fruit Salad with a Lemon Jelly

(SERVES 6–8)

1 cup fresh lemon juice 30 g gelatine	Put juice in a bowl and sprinkle gelatine over the top. Whisk well and set aside.
$3\frac{1}{2}$ cups water 1 cup caster sugar 1 tspn grated fresh lemon rind	Place in a pot, bring to the boil, regularly stirring, and cook until sugar has dissolved. Then pour into above mix and whisk until gelatine has dissolved.
$^{3}/_{4}$ cup fresh lemon juice	Add, whisk again and put into dariole moulds. Cool, cover and refrigerate for 1–2 hours until set.
a selection of fresh fruit such as mango, kiwifruit, banana, strawberries, passionfruit	Prepare as necessary and cut into even chunks.
orange liqueur	Toss salad with orange liqueur and when jellies are set, unmould onto flat soup bowls and serve fruit salad around.

'This fresh, tart jelly is wonderful with fresh fruit (or by itself).'

Tea-Poached Dates

(SERVES 6–8)

1 cup sugar	Boil for 5 minutes and then remove tea bags.
2 cups water	
2 Earl Grey tea bags	
2 cardamon pods	
1 vanilla bean, split	
3–4 dozen pitted dates	Add and poach very gently for 2–3 minutes.
200 g mascarpone	Mix together and serve on top of dates –
grated zest of 1 orange	hot or cold.
orange juice to taste	

 'I was very pleasantly surprised by this simple dessert – it's terrific.'

Lumberjack Cake

(SERVES 8–10)

cooking spray baking paper	Preheat oven to 170°C. Spray a 20 cm round springform cake tin and line base with baking paper.
200 g dates, pitted & chopped 1 tspn bicarb of soda 2 large Granny Smith apples, peeled, cored & grated	Put in a bowl and mix. Then pour over 1 cup of boiling water, mix again and set aside until warm.
125 g unsalted butter 1 tspn vanilla essence 1 cup sugar	Beat, with an electric mixer until light and creamy.
1 large egg 1½ cups plain flour, sifted	Add egg and beat until combined. Then stir in date mix and fold in sifted flour until just combined and almost smooth. Spoon into tin and cook in oven for 40 minutes.
1 cup desiccated coconut ½ cup brown sugar 75 g unsalted butter ½ cup milk	Combine in a small pot and gently cook until butter is melted and ingredients are well combined. Remove cake from oven, spread over the top and cook for another 30 minutes until top is golden. Cool in tin before turning out.

'Whenever I make this, I find myself humming the Monty Python song which has lines like 'I'm a lumberjack and I'm OK. I wear high heels and I drink all day' – or words to that effect. (I have never been terribly good at remembering the words to songs.)'

Poached Fresh Pears with Lemon Ricotta and a Honey & Passionfruit Sauce

(SERVES 4–6)

1 litre sugar syrup (equal quantities of sugar & water boiled until sugar dissolves)
juice of 1 lemon
1 cinnamon stick
4 cloves

Put in a pot and bring to the boil.

4–6 pears, peeled, cored & halved

Put in syrup, gently place plate on top and simmer very slowly for 15 minutes or so until tender. Set aside to cool in liquid.

200 g ricotta
2 heaped tbsp icing sugar
$1/4$ tspn vanilla essence
grated zest of 1 lemon
fresh lemon juice

Mix together, adding lemon juice to taste.

4 tbsp honey
pulp of 5–6 passionfruit
juice of 1 lemon

Heat in a small pot.

Place pears on plates, mound ricotta mix on top and drizzle with sauce.

'Just between you and me, this works rather well with canned pear halves – but only those which have been preserved in natural syrup.'

Hi
Hewy – Baby!

Hope you enjoy these:
Why do they wait until a pig is dead to 'cure' it?
Is it true that cannibals don't eat clowns
because they taste funny?
If a parsley farmer is sued, can they garnish his
wages?
Why do they call it a TV set when you only
have one?
What was the best thing before sliced bread?
David NSW

Loved your Chicken Niçoise but I must tell you that the above spelling is
pronounced 'nee-swahz' and not 'nee-swah'. 'SE' makes the 'S' pronounced.
If there was no 'e' on the end it would be a silent 'S' – 'swah'. Please note the 'E'.
Anon

Can you please send me the recipe for your beetroot relish? My sister got it off
your show and she won't share it with anyone.
Emma NSW

Some recipes call for one or two anchovies. I am only cooking for one so it
seems a waste to open a can when I might not get around to eating the rest.
I have enclosed a packet from a paste that I like. Can I substitute this for an
anchovy from a can? If so, how much do I use?
Mrs H NSW

Chocolate & Ginger Ice Box Cake

(SERVES 6–8)

900 g plain chocolate biscuits	Crumble in a processor and put in a large bowl.
140 g room temperature unsalted butter, cubed $1/2$ tspn ground ginger	Add to bowl and, using your hands, rub together until the mixture has the texture of coarse breadcrumbs.
cooking spray	Lightly spray a 20 cm springform tin.
1 cup yoghurt 1 cup crystallised ginger, finely chopped 400 g soft cream cheese 1 tspn vanilla essence 1 cup chocolate buttons, roughly chopped $1^1/3$ cups sugar	Put in a separate bowl and carefully mix with a hand-held electric beater.
$3/4$ cup cream 900 g mascarpone	Add and gently whip, being careful not to overbeat.
	Place half the biscuit mix into tin, spread half of mascarpone-ginger cream on top and then repeat process, finishing with a thin layer of crumbs. Tightly cover with kitchen wrap and refrigerate overnight.

 'Using this recipe as your blueprint, vary it to suit your own likes and dislikes.'

Italian Rice Pudding

(SERVES 4–6)

600 ml milk	Preheat oven to 180°C.
100 ml cream	Put in a pot and simmer for 10 minutes.
140 g caster sugar	
120 g risotto rice	
1 tbsp sultanas	Add and simmer for another 10 minutes.
1 tbsp dried apricots, diced	
1 tbsp glace pineapple, diced	
1 tbsp glace ginger, diced	
a splash of vanilla extract	
4 large eggs, beaten	Add and mix well. Then pour into a
¼ cup orange liqueur	greased baking dish and cook in oven
grated zest of 1 lemon	for 30–40 minutes.
icing sugar	Cool a little, then generously dust with icing sugar and glaze top with a mini blowtorch.

'My mother always made a wonderful, yet rather basic rice pudding. I hate to say it but this is even better (and a lot fancier too).'

Xmas Ice-Cream Pudding

(SERVES 10 PLUS)

2 cups mixed dried fruits 100 g glace pineapple, chopped 100 g glace cherries, chopped 50 g glace ginger, chopped finely grated zest of 2 oranges $3/4$ cup chocolate bits 2 tbsp brandy 2 tbsp grand marnier	Mix together.
4 litres softened, bought vanilla ice-cream	Add and mix in well. Then line an extra large bowl with kitchen wrap, spoon in the mix and cover with more wrap. Place in freezer overnight and, when required, remove top piece of wrap, invert over a serving plate and wrap a hot towel around it to help it come out.
a mixture of berries Grand Marnier icing sugar	Serve with berries which have been tossed in Grand Marnier and dust with icing sugar.

'Always one of our most popular recipes. Last year on Radio Station 3AW, I made the mistake of telling a listener that the producer had the recipe (which he didn't) and blocked the lines for well over an hour, as seemingly everyone in the world rang in wanting it. The producers were not terribly happy because, apart from answering the phone continually, there was little or no talkback that morning as the lines were taken up by requests for my 'bloody' Ice-Cream Pudding.'

QUICK REFERENCE

Dear Mr Hewtsen

Our grade was so excited to get another letter from you.
You have all of our permission to use any of our letters
in your new book. That is so exciting!
We think you're the best chef on TV. We made the
chocolate cornflake recipe you showed us and we all
enjoyed them. We made so many our teacher must have
got the measurements wrong but we were happy.
Keep on cooking and smiling.
Good luck with your new book.

Your Grade 4/5 friends at St Mary Magdalen's

CONVERSION TABLES

The conversions below are workable approximates for the metric measurements given in the recipes.

★ OVEN TEMPERATURES

60°C	120°F	Very slow
150°C	300°F	Slow
180°C	350°F	Moderate
200°C	400°F	Moderately hot
230°C	450°F	Hot
250°C	500°F	Very hot

★ WEIGHT MEASUREMENTS

Metric	Imperial
15 g	$^1/_2$ oz
30 g	1 oz
60 g	2 oz
90 g	3 oz
120 g	4 oz ($^1/_4$ lb)
150 g	5 oz
180 g	6 oz
200 g	7 oz
250 g	8 oz ($^1/_2$ lb)
300 g	10 oz
345 g	11 oz
375 g	12 oz ($^3/_4$ lb)
400 g	14 oz
500 g	16 oz (1 lb)
750 g	$1^1/_2$ lb
1 kg	about 2 lb
1.5 kg	about 3 lb
2 kg	4 lb 6 oz

★ VOLUME MEASUREMENTS

Metric	Imperial	US Cups
15 ml	$^1/_2$ fl oz	1 tablespoon
30 ml	1 fl oz	
60 ml	2 fl oz	$^1/_4$ cup
100 ml	$3^1/_2$ fl oz	
125 ml	4 fl oz	$^1/_2$ cup
150 ml	5 fl oz ($^1/_4$ pint)	$^2/_3$ cup
175 ml	6 fl oz	$^3/_4$ cup
200 ml	7 fl oz	
250 ml	8 fl oz	1 cup ($^1/_2$ pint)
300 ml	10 fl oz ($^1/_2$ pint)	
375 ml	12 fl oz	$1^1/_2$ cups
400 ml	13 fl oz	
500 ml	16 fl oz	2 cups (1 pint)
600 ml	1 pint (20 fl oz)	$2^1/_2$ cups
750 ml	24 fl oz	3 cups
1.25 lt	2 pints	4 cups (1 quart)
2 lt	$3^1/_4$ pints	$6^1/_3$ cups
2.5 lt	4 pints	8 cups

★ MEASURES

3 mm	$^1/_8$ in
1 cm	$^1/_3$ in
2 cm	$^3/_4$ in
5 cm	2 in
15 cm	6 in
21.5 cm	8 in

Index